THE NEW
MARKETING ERA

THE NEW MARKETING ERA

Marketing to the Imagination in a Technology-Driven World

Paul Postma

McGraw-Hill
New York   San Francisco   Washington, D.C.   Auckland   Bogotá
Caracas   Lisbon   London   Madrid   Mexico City   Milan
Montreal   New Delhi   San Juan   Singapore
Sydney   Tokyo   Toronto

Library of Congress Cataloging-in-Publication Data

Postma, Paul.
    The new marketing era : marketing to the imagination in a
technology driven world / Paul Postma.
       p.   cm.
    Includes bibliographical references and index.
    ISBN 0-07-052675-3
    1. Marketing—Technological innovations. 2. Marketing—
Psychological aspects. 3. Consumer behavior. I. Title.
HF5415.P642   1998
658.8—dc21   98-34857
                                           CIP

McGraw-Hill

A Division of The **McGraw·Hill** Companies

1 2 3 4 5 6 7 8 9 0   FGR/FGR   9 0 3 2 1 0 9 8

ISBN 0-07-052675-3

*The editing supervisor was Caroline Levine and the production
supervisor was Sherri Souffrance. This book was set in Fairfield by
Victoria Khavkina of McGraw-Hill's Professional Book Group
composition unit.*

Printed and bound by Quebecor/Fairfield.

McGraw-Hill books are available at special quantity discounts to
use as premiums and sales promotions, or for use in corporate
training programs. For more information, please write to the
Director of Special Sales, McGraw-Hill, 11 West 19th Street, New
York, NY 10011. Or contact your local bookstore.

 This book is printed on recycled, acid-free paper containing
a minimum of 50% recycled, de-inked fiber.

CONTENTS

FOREWORD

The Future remains an open question that each marketer has to try to answer. On the eve of the twenty-first century, in the turbulent nineties which are characterized by a series of fundamental social, technological, and economic changes, this is not an easy task. We are moving into the new marketing era. We are not sure of the rate at which we are moving into the new world economy and high-tech economy, but it is happening. We have to make a special effort to figure out what tomorrow looks like and move toward it.

What's new in the way of media? There used to be five: magazines, newspapers, billboards, radio, and television. They have been around for a long time and will continue to be used. But now we've got to get into direct mail, telephone marketing, audio and video tapes, and multimedia CD-ROMs, Internet, Intranet, commercial on-line services, and e-mail and fax-mail on demand as selling tools.

However, I have found that whenever there is something new, it doesn't replace the old—it's just another layer. Television did not kill radio, nor did it kill newspapers. There was instead a reorganization of the strength of these media. Although the future belongs increasingly to database marketing, there are lot of marketing models operating. Thus we see the coexistence of different ways to win.

Watch your competitors; they probably have home pages now, and that means you should get started, too. The key issues are how to make a good Web page and how to get people to look at your page.

Don't think "business as usual," because there is a great

new world of new media out there. Think about being two kinds of marketer. First, put your company on the Internet very strongly, so that people can get information readily. Second, go into database marketing so that you can learn a lot about your customers. You will be protected because you're on the Internet and customers will learn about your offering and buy from you. At the same time you will know about your customers' needs and, through database marketing, propose offers that will help them.

Our literature has it that we are very cognitive and have "computer brains" to enable us to make the best choice. Paul Postma reminds us in *The New Marketing Era* that we have a primitive, animal side—for better or worse. He raises questions about the role of database marketing and Internet, and their impact on human nature and marketing.

Paul Postma is one of those rare marketing thinkers whose deep technical knowledge and psychological insights make him a perfect guide to illuminate for "old era marketers" the rich opportunities which are being opened up by the new electronic media.

Philip Kotler
S.C. Johnson & Son
Distinguished Professor of International Marketing
Northwestern University

PREFACE

The revolution that is currently taking place in information technology, and its exploitation by the media, has turned the marketing world upside down. Today's marketers are finding it hard to appreciate the extent of its impact on the marketing process. There is, however, one essential factor that is often ignored: human behavior has been determined by the same mental processes for millions of years. While forms of expression may certainly mutate, the age-old behavior patterns, with their origins in the human nervous system itself, remain the same. In a high-tech economy, the persistence of these primal patterns can be quite surprising.

Following an introductory chapter, *The New Marketing Era* will describe the revolutions occurring respectively in information technology and the media. After describing their technical aspects, we will discuss the relevance of these upheavals in the context of marketing. If you are already familiar with these technical developments, you can probably skim over the first four sections of Chapter 2 and the second section of Chapter 3.

Human behavior is the essence of marketing. Chapter 4, "We're only human," looks at the way in which people appear to absorb information and how they form decisions on the basis of the information gathered; we examine how people perceive the media and react to it. This behavior is then analyzed within the context of the workings of the human mind, with its age-old brain systems and their functions. In the final chapter, the mutual influence of information, media, and human beings will be considered within the larger overall framework of business and commerce.

I hope that reading this old-fashioned medium will be a pleasurable experience. Your reactions are most welcome. My address is: nlpostm3@mey.nl.

ACKNOWLEDGMENTS

It would not have been possible to write this book without the work on marketing strategy that we have carried out for our clients, which include leading marketing-oriented multinationals. I would like to express my grateful thanks to them. I would also like to thank the persons mentioned in the references for their insights. In addition I wish to thank NCR's Hans Molenaar; Irdeto's Peter Vossen; Compaq's Rhod Smith; SAS Institute's Phil Winters; Dr. Steven Schoemaker, who is responsible for the implementation of new technologies at the ING Barings; and the eminent neurologist, Professor S.A.J. de Froe, for his advice on the passages about the human mind. I would especially like to thank Professor Philip Kotler for our interesting discussions and his encouragement to publish this English language edition of *The New Marketing Era*. Finally, my grateful thanks to my wife Hanneke and my children Elger, Nienke, and Wiegertje for their enduring patience during the vacations that I have devoted to the preparation of this book.

Paul Postma

MARKETING IN A CHANGING WORLD

In this first chapter we will look at how technical developments are taking hold of many aspects of our daily lives, particularly in commercial transactions. In this new marketing era, established marketing concepts seem to be assuming a completely different meaning; the ways of viewing the market and the possibilities of influencing it are taking on a new dimension. Technology plays a decisive role, but the human factor always remains the same. *In the last 25 years the processing power of the silicon chip has increased ten thousand fold; the processing power of the human brain has remained the same.* An unusual problem results.

WAITING IN A TRAFFIC JAM FOR THE ELECTRONIC HIGHWAY

Technology is making our lives more convenient and comfortable. At the same time, our lives are becoming more complex, more confusing, and sometimes even treacherous. Both developments are a result of the same thing: technology.

We no longer poke the coals in the fireplace in order to warm our house; we simply tape the thermostat and let technology do the rest. The clatter of pots on ceramic tiles has been replaced by the purr of the dishwasher. We can zap from the latest world news to a drama series, game show, or sports event. When we drive to work, we simply select the temperature that we find most comfortable. It doesn't matter whether it is bitingly cold or sweltering hot outside—technology takes care of it for us. While driving to work, we can already make our first business calls. The fax confirming the appointment reaches the office before we do, and the comments of a colleague abroad are already posted on the network. All this is happening even before the arrival of the electronic highway. These are the blessings of technology.

There is a downside as well. Technology seems to be powerless when it comes to a fluctuating economy, social upheaval, and natural disasters such as earthquakes, cyclones, and floods. Didn't the 1995 floods in the river deltas of northern France, Belgium, and Holland occur despite all the technical tricks that led us to believe they couldn't happen? Or was it actually partly a result of technological progress that the rivers broke their banks? Some natural disasters, such as the earthquakes in California and Japan, have the power to destroy a technology-based infrastructure in a matter of seconds. Even without such a calamity and with a perfectly functioning infrastructure, it still takes us more than an hour to drive the 20 miles from home to work in our air-conditioned cars that were, incidentally, designed to reach speeds of up to 150 miles/hour. Meanwhile, we're sitting there waiting for the electronic highway. Now, what did we say about those technological blessings?

Our lives have altered radically in just a few decades. The changes have only just started. Technology has made physical strain, far from being a necessity of daily life, to being a voluntary luxury that keeps us in shape. On the other hand, we are confronted with new situations that we don't really know how to deal with. Similarly, we have to face the fact that in the event of a power outage the entire office shuts down; 20 years ago, work would have carried on as usual. Then we have that remarkable annual phenomenon of the whole country grinding to a standstill at the first sign of ice or snow. Nobody can go anywhere, even though today's cars are fitted with high-tech equipment. Finally, despite all that talk about a paperless society, we've never had as much paper in our lives. At least that goes for the "haves" among us, because the gap with the have-nots is becoming increasingly noticeable.

The landscape has changed completely—not necessarily for better or worse—and the new contours present new challenges. It is as if you were on a train moving across Europe from north to south. The lowlands of the north gradually become more hilly; a few hours later the outline of mountains looms like a dark cloud in the distance, and before you know it you are traveling through them. If you doze for a few hours, you will hardly be able to believe your eyes when you wake up. If your attention wanders for just a moment, you'll wake up to find that everything around you has changed.

INFORMATION AND MEDIA ARE TRANSFORMING THE MARKETING ENVIRONMENT

In the new marketing era, we look at these developments through the eyes of a marketer: through the eyes of a businessperson who traces and manages markets in order to achieve economic transactions. We judge the changing markets, not from a political or technological viewpoint, but purely in the light of the consequences for commerce. And these are very far-reaching.

For us, marketing means the whole commercial process leading to economic exchange. In terms of the new marketing era, marketing can be understood as the transmission and reception of communication impulses with the ultimate aim of receiving sales impulses. It is within this framework that everything to do with marketing takes place: product, price setting, promotion, contacts, branding, service, and distribution. And this whole commercial process depends on the communication of information.

How has the marketing profession itself developed in the last decade? A lot has been published on this topic in recent years.[1] A determining factor in these changes is the diminishing importance of traditional marketing-mix instruments such as the four Ps—product, price, place, and promotion—popularized by McCarthy.[2] It is becoming apparent that these instruments are no longer sufficient in rapidly changing markets. By using specially created marketing databases, however, the possibilities of effectively influencing the market increase quite considerably—as long as the data satisfy the necessary criteria. Technology places us in a much better position to apply an individual approach even in very large markets, thanks to the facts about clients and prospects that have been compiled in the database. Initially this meant personalized mass communication, with the same message sent to individually addressed people. Now large-scale personalized mass communication is being applied, with the message specifically tailored to the known characteristics of the individual recipient. As a result, activities in the business market can be more sharply focused and mass marketing in consumer markets can be complemented, and sometimes replaced, by one-to-one marketing. Thus information at a product/client level supersedes the more generic models and assumptions.

In addition to the emphasis placed on brand, considerable attention is given to customer care, to the relationship with the individual client. Brand management is still important, but so too is customer service management. Both have become essential aspects of marketing. The cost-effectiveness of the traditional mass-marketing strategies has been further decreased by the diversification of the media and consumer groups. *This doesn't mean that mass marketing is dead, but rather that it is of far less significance.* Customers are no longer prepared to take things at face value. Individual behavior can no longer be deduced by defining the target group to which that person belongs. The relationship with the critical and mature client is now the number-one priority for the marketer.[3]

Technological developments make it possible for us to allow clients to react to the supplier, and to make their wishes and preferences known. The one-way bombardment by the supplier is giving way to a dialogue between supplier and consumer. It is no longer the supplier that calls the shots and the client that swallows everything without question; today's client makes demands to which the company listens and reacts. The individual relationship based on data in marketing databases can be achieved because technological developments not only make large-scale use of data a possibility but also create a new dimension for communication between supplier and purchaser. Using media to convey a message occupies an increasingly important place in creating effective economic transactions.

In the period of predominantly mass marketing, companies used the media primarily for advertising. Consider, for example, thematic advertising. In today's changing marketing world, the media are increasingly used to establish one-to-one relationships with clients and prospects. In this way, the medium as data carrier assumes a completely new dimension in the commercial process. This difference is illustrated in Figure 1-1.

We can now define the *new marketing era* as characterized by three points:

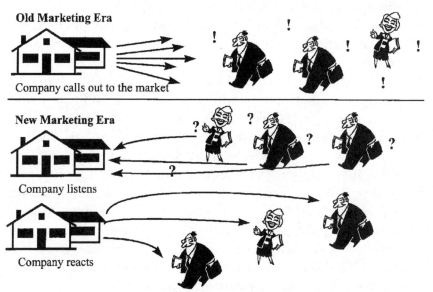

FIGURE 1-1. One-sided bombardment is replaced by dialogue.

- Marketing management according to the information held in marketing databases rather than that acquired through market research and generic models
- The use of media instead of generic (thematic) advertising to stimulate trade
- Management of personal client relationships as opposed to management of more or less defined target groups

We should realize that established marketing techniques such as marketing-mix models, target groups, and advertising will remain, but new approaches will emerge alongside them and, in an increasing number of cases, will eventually overtake them. Mass marketing will not disappear but will lose its dominant position.

IMPACT ON BUSINESS MARKETS

As we have seen, two developments enable us to build a client relationship: one from the field of information and one from the field of media. Their effects apply equally to business-to-business markets and business-to-consumer (retail) markets. The dissimilarities with the old situation are, however, different in each case.

Superficially, the evolution toward the new marketing era in business markets seems to entail less of an upheaval than in consumer markets. This is because business markets have never been quite so extreme as consumer markets in considering customers as a relatively anonymous group. The distance between the supplier (manufacturer, dealer, or importer) and the buyer is often less than in the consumer-goods market. The director of a medium-size enterprise in business-to-business markets soon gets to know all the main customers and visits them in person. Sales representatives maintain personal contact with the customer network so there is little risk of the supplier and the customer getting out of touch.

Nonetheless, the growing impact of information and the

media is just as evident here—particularly when suppliers, whether of goods or services, tend to place their own product above anything else. The manufacturer, builder, or service provider can be so enthusiastic about its own product or service that it completely forgets about the customer. Typical comments: "Customers don't know what they need." "The client has no idea how complex it is to deliver a particular service." "The client has no taste." "The client isn't prepared to pay for quality." These are just some examples of how suppliers are more concerned with themselves than with the customers they're supposed to be doing it all for.

We have to ask whether clients really don't know what they want or whether suppliers simply don't listen to their clients' wishes. The complexities involved in delivering a product are the supplier's problem, not the client's. As regards taste, we often come across service suppliers with a certain degree of artistic input in, say, architecture and design who are hardnosed about their own style even when it is not in keeping with the client's requirements. The professional and intellectual pride of accountants and lawyers often clouds their view of the market. The fruits of the information revolution can help correct the view of the market in the professional arenas. Product orientation can be turned into—or at least complemented by—a strong customer orientation.

A second point of importance in the business-to-business markets is that the media can exert greater influence in those markets where sales representatives have become too costly. New media developments have taken over a growing number of the traditional tasks of sales representatives or advisers. This is particularly true for the selection of prospects and also for certain product areas. Office supplies can be sold very well via database-operated catalogs; standard office furniture presents more problems, but it can be sold in this way in certain circumstances. A sales representative is still required for customized office fittings, but the profit margins and turnover can absorb the extra cost. Just imagine ordering a custom-made office through the electronic media. Virtual reality can provide a far better idea of that office than a sketch made by a rep.

A third development is that suppliers can now publicize their range of products or services electronically so that prospects can make their own buying decisions. Used in this way, the new media serve the same function as trade shows or exhibitions that enable prospects to compare all the products or services available in a certain market. But the electronic trade show is a permanent exhibition. There's only one danger. Depending on the medium, dissatisfied clients can voice their objections to the world. Obviously there has to be sufficient control.

All these developments point toward drastic changes in the business market landscape, and survival will depend on successful adaptation. The business services sector will be most deeply affected.

IMPACT ON CONSUMER MARKETS

For many, the new marketing era will have a greater impact on consumer markets than on business markets. In these markets, the mass-marketing approach is often supplemented or partially replaced by an individual approach.

The character of information is changing radically in consumer markets. You can read about the changes later in this chapter and in Chapter 2. It is now possible to determine what the actual consumption and preferences of certain consumers are, rather than having to depend on lists of target group characteristics or on what customers say their preferences are. For many consumer goods, whether they are chocolate bars or packaged soups, reported brand popularity is often totally at odds with actual market share. Devising strategies based on brand name and declared brand preferences seems to lie farther from commercial reality than has long been supposed. Recent developments in information gathering enable us to look behind reported preferences and brand perception at the actual purchasing behavior of each client. The emphasis shifts from *what* passes the checkout counter to *who takes what* past the checkout counter. Thus, both retail and consumer brand suppliers can get a clearer picture of the market, which is very much on a par with the situation in business markets described in the previous section.

As a result of these developments, the media are gaining influence in a large number of areas—except, perhaps, the area that has been the subject of most speculation: teleshopping. Although teleshopping is an important option for services such as insurance, banking, and travel, and for mail-order companies, it poses significant drawbacks for weekly grocery shopping. It is often far better to have the customer collect certain goods than to deliver them.

In markets where the lion's share of purchases is made by relatively few people, the new marketing era offers the opportunity for considerable progress. Since only relatively few people are responsible for the major share of the turnover, these customers can be approached individually. In consumer markets, the insight into this all-important point is fairly recent. Studies have shown that even among normal fast-moving consumer goods like soft drinks, the number of buyers that create a profit for the supplier is surprisingly low. Their preferences shift easily among three brands. Gaining these customers' loyalty should be a high priority.[4] Marketing schemes, described as customer loyalty programs, can prevent these important clients from leaving by the back door immediately after they step through the front door—and it often takes a good deal of effort and money to get them that far.

The media therefore make it possible to establish a personal relationship with customers in mass consumer markets in a way that was previously close to impossible on any significant scale. The use of new electronic media more or less automatically results in the collection of data, a by-product that can be of considerable value to management: The various shopping programs on television and the on-line ordering facilities on the Internet are examples. The new media can also provide fresh insight into classical marketing strategies by reinforcing brand awareness and by using quiz questions to generate data and customer loyalty.

In sum, the changing landscape is a good reason for reappraising the merits of marketing policies for both business and consumer markets. Missing the bandwagon is just as bad as jumping on too soon.

INFORMATION IS CHANGING

Those who think the changing nature of information is irrelevant because market information has always been important are missing the point. Of course market research companies have been around for decades. Tests and questionnaires are administered, and exhaustive desk research is carried out using every possible source of information. We shouldn't think all this will disappear or become redundant. As with every new phenomenon, there is always something novel that overshadows the importance of previous variants. In this case it is a type of information that may seem run of the mill to outsiders but that has a totally different value for marketers.

It is the difference between information that tells us about brand awareness and purported preferences and information that tells us about actual purchasing behavior. It is the difference between what we say in a telephone interview and what we actually do. For example, we could be stopped on arrival at an airport by a friendly market researcher who asks us questions about how frequently we travel, continentally and intercontinentally, in which class, and on which airline. Most of us are considerate enough to take a few moments to reply. At the same time, our thoughts are elsewhere. We're thinking about our family or about our luggage. Only when we are in the car on the way home do we realize that our last trip to Japan was actually much longer ago than we said. If we want to know the exact travel details of particular customers, we shouldn't ask them. Rather, we must find out when they bought their tickets, from whom, and when they checked in for which destination. *There can be an extraordinary disparity between the information given and actual behavior.* This is also true when questionnaires contain every possible control question and are completely divested of any influence of social correctness—for example, by asking for projections about other people.

Modern technology provides far more cost-effective methods of pinpointing actual behavior instead of reported behavior. Reported totals are frequently considerably at odds with actual totals, and stated preferences are hardly ever translated into actual sales. After all, revenue is generated only by sales—not by stated preferences. This sales behavior contains consistent patterns that, within defined parameters, can be used to predict future buying behavior. This phenomenon, and the reasons for it, is discussed in greater depth in Chapter 2.

The consequences of such disparity are more profound than they may at first appear. Marketing managers, just like everyone else, tend to believe facts that seem self-evident. For example, expensive goods are bought by people with plenty of money, and the cheaper variants are purchased by the less affluent. Brand-new Jaguars are certainly the reserve of the wealthy, but the pattern does not hold for grocery shopping. The figures do not bear out the notion that people with high incomes buy the more expensive brands. Similarly, expensive insurance companies find that their principal markets are not in the higher-income groups. By the same token, cheap, direct underwriters do not find that their clients are mainly from the low-income groups. The premiums of insurance companies that successfully target the bottom end of the market using salaried representatives are anything but cheap.

Those who study the actual patterns of purchasing behavior will discover that reality is often totally different from the impression given by careful market research based on the responses to questionnaires. *The well-heeled are also attracted by bargains, reductions, and promotional offers.* The largest Dutch mail-order company for flower bulbs did not add the variable "with or without garden" to its database—something that would have been easy—because doing so apparently made no difference to the likelihood of someone buying bulbs. A major English mail-order company, with an assortment comparable to that of a department store, confirms that there is no relation whatsoever between customers making a purchase from the gardening section and whether those customers have a garden or not. Banks have no problem selling off capital products designed for customers who fall into the highest tax bracket to clients who fall outside it. The famous saying "The product was a success, but not with the customers for whom it was intended" fully expresses this misconception.

The possibilities of collecting data have everything to do with the new media. People using the electronic highway as a means of communication automatically leave traces of their activities behind. Companies that receive such communications may, within the bounds of privacy laws, retain those traces and use them for further communication. *These tracks are as personal as those left by wild animals; they show the way to the watering hole.* And anybody who discovers these tracks can sit back and wait until the animals return for their next drink. We have more in common with animals than all our intellectual knowledge would lead us to believe.

MEDIA ARE CHANGING

All that has been said about the new function of information in the new marketing era also applies to the function of media. At first glance, the difference between the traditional forms of media used in marketing and the new applications is not particularly striking. Once the difference is recognized, though, we need to be careful not to reach the standard conclusion that all the old forms of media will be totally superseded by the new.

Media or information carriers are the means to accomplish or transmit something. They can be newspapers or television stations. Media are used for many different purposes. They carry news, are the playing field for politics, and offer a whole variety of entertainment—from crossword puzzles to gossip columns, from quizzes to game shows. They form a platform and means of communication for culture, and media are used for marketing purposes.

The most common use of media for commercial purposes is advertising. At the start of the century these were little more than simple announcements about items for sale or about the arrival of a new batch of a particular product. Advertising now forms a crucial aspect of economic activity in every developed economy, with markets in the United States, Canada, and Europe in the hundreds of billions of dollars. Traditionally, a distinction is made between above-the-line advertising—that which appears in newspapers, magazines, and movie theaters and on radio, TV, and billboards—and below-the-line activities, including direct mail, sales promotions, sponsoring, and exhibitions or trade shows. Around 40 percent is spent on above-the-line advertising with the balance on below-the-line. The latter category is increasing at a slightly faster rate.

Advertising has various functions, but its chief aim remains that of attracting the attention of the readers or viewers of a medium. The purpose can be that of spreading information about special offers (promotional advertising), attracting customers to a shop, praising the quality of a range of goods, simply drawing attention to the existence of the advertiser, or creating or underlining the image of a product, group of products, brand, or company. A substantial part of advertising money is spent on the latter—namely, the launching, strengthening, or development of a brand image. When we talk about media use in the new marketing era, however, we are no longer talking about this form of media. The boundary lies where advertising agencies rightly claim that it is their responsibility to increase product or service awareness, but not to sell. The effect of advertising cannot be measured in terms of extra sales or the number of new customers, nor is this required. We won't discuss that here.

When we talk about the functions of media in the commercial process in the new marketing era, we are referring to those functions that produce tangible, quantifiable results. These are the areas where media assume a role comparable to that of sales representatives, or where they replace shops, markets, and trade fairs. The return on investment made in these instruments can be measured in terms of clients, orders, margin, or turnover.

In order to clarify the position of media in commercial processes, let us look at three principal ways in which

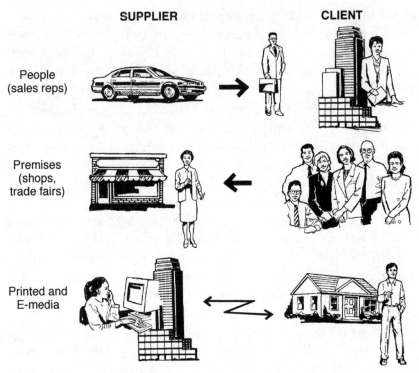

SUPPLIER   CLIENT

People
(sales reps)

Premises
(shops,
trade fairs)

Printed and
E-media

FIGURE 1-2.   The three measurable marketing methods.

those processes can be constructed.[5] These are illustrated in Figure 1-2.

1. The supplier—the company—can visit potential buyers, customers, and prospects. Salespeople, advisors, or other representatives are given this job. They are the modern day equivalent of the peddler who sold wares door-to-door. We call this possibility *people*.

2. The buyer—the client—can also go in search of potential suppliers. In terms of who goes in search of whom, this is the direct opposite of item 1. Here it is the client who moves around rather than the supplier. Formerly, the client would visit warehouses and annual markets; these days, the client visits shops, exhibitions, and markets. In fact, they visit either a fixed or mobile location where suppliers offer their wares. This possibility is known as *place*.

3. Neither party visits the other directly; instead, the parties communicate in print or electronically. Information is sent via a data carrier or medium. This possibility is called *media,* and it includes both print and electronic media. This is the media function we are concerned with in the new marketing era.

If the telephone is used structurally in the commercial process as a medium with (partially) predetermined dialogues, then this application has so many features in common with other means of communication that we can consider it a form of media. At a call center, the incoming and outgoing calls are supported by a database, and this makes a predetermined dialogue seem very personal. During the session the name and relevant details appear on the computer screen of the "agent" or caller—which is why we consider telemarketing as one of the possible media, even when the telephone is answered by a person. These forms of computer integrated telephony (CIT) already play an enormous role in the realization of mass personal communication, and are expected to grow considerably. If the phone is answered by a voice-response system, it can be considered an even purer form of media, since it works without any human intervention.

People, place, and media form three *measurable marketing methods* that can facilitate the economic trading process, whether alone or in combination. Most organizations use one of them as their chief method, complemented by one or both of the others. For example, a trading business approaches the industrial market with representatives (people), but once every two years it also takes a strand at the trade fair (place). A clothing company sells to the customer via a chain of shops (place), and in addition has a direct-mail program (media) for its best clients. An insurer sells as a direct writer (media) to the consumer, but employs sales reps (people) for the business market. *The balance among these three measurable marketing methods is one of the most important strategic choices in the marketing process.*

When we talk about media in the new marketing era, we are referring to the media in its function as sketched above.

This is direct marketing, or the execution of the marketing process, or parts thereof, using electronic and/or printed information carriers without human intervention. The current English language definitions are broader, encompassing every media possibility, but still they amount to the same thing. Consider this definition from 1983, when direct marketing was still primarily restricted to mail-order companies and the possible uses for other media were only just starting to develop: "orders placed by mail, phone, or electronically without the person ordering coming to the point of sale to place the order or the seller coming to the office or home of the orderer to take the order or using an agent to collect the order."[6] In short, even then direct marketing referred to its core—doing business via the media. Since then that core of possibilities has grown considerably.

The media are subject to developments that are just as rapid as those taking place in information technology, and are also driven by technology; it is the client that will ultimately decide whether a development will be accepted. When we describe the media as information carriers, it is obvious that media and information are two aspects of the same development. This development is the reason that media—the information as much as the carrier—will continue to play such a rapidly increasing role in the whole marketing process. It is also possible to claim that media and information are becoming more important for the whole of society, and that commercial activity as a part of that society is no exception.

The media can fulfill a broad range of functions in the commercial process. Figure 1-3 illustrates the functions of media according to two characteristics: those including all or part of the product range, and those including the whole commercial process (e.g., the traditional mail-order business) or part of that process.

Growth is to be found not so much in the top left quadrant of Figure 1-3—companies that perform the whole commercial process for their total range of products—as in the other three quadrants. For items in the product range where personal selling is becoming too expensive, doing business via the media

		Product range	
		Whole	**Part**
Commercial process	**Whole**	• **Mail order companies** e.g., Kays, 3 Suisses • **Conference organizers** e.g., Euroforum, Frost & Sullivan • **Lotteries** e.g., National Lottery • **Financial services** e.g., American Express, First Direct, VISA	• **Computer supplies** e.g., IBM Direct • **Insurers and financial services** e.g., AA and RAC, Virgin Insurance
	Part	• **Car importers and dealers** Coupons and mailings to leads e.g., Volvo, Rover, Ford • **Shops and airlines** Cards to establish customer loyalty e.g., Marks & Spencer, Harvey Nichols, United Airlines	• **Brand manufacturers** Coupons and mailings to heavy users e.g., Procter & Gamble for diapers • **Banks and building societies** Mailing and telemarketing to establish leads and client contacts e.g., Barclays, NatWest

FIGURE 1-3.   Direct Marketing Matrix of Applications.

presents an attractive alternative. (See the top right quadrant of Figure 1-3.) The establishment of a safe method of payment via these same media is an important precondition for success. Strong growth is occurring in the bottom half of the matrix, where media are used in certain parts of the commercial process. Finding the right prospects and maintaining customer relations with the best clients can be excellently managed with data-driven media. Since media combined with data management offer more and more possibilities, the end of this expansion is not yet in sight.

What in fact is happening is that, thanks to business being conducted via media, the personal relationships from the era of the peddler are once again returning. Of course, the supplier comes to the door in the form of data communication. And if at all possible the supplier is better informed than the peddler of yesteryear. The mass approach that encouraged ever larger shops is now waning because of developments in information technology.

RELATIONS MAKE THE WORLD GO ROUND

With the aid of information and media, marketing management can be considerably more sophisticated than it was with the traditional means. In the old marketing era, sales representatives, shops, and trade shows dealt at best with assumed or logically deduced target groups. As has already been indicated, information and media can now perform a totally different commercial function in the new marketing era.

Given that media are becoming more and more effective in influencing the senses (see the following chapters) and given that media management takes on a whole new dimension through the use of data, the trading process can now increasingly occur without personal intervention, even though it is still possible to create excellent relationships. Reacting to the personal behavior of customers or prospects by responding to their obvious interests with an electronic message, a letter, a brochure, or an offer actually fosters clients' feeling that you are becoming acquainted with their tastes and preferences, and are taking them into consideration.

In addition, loyal customers will value being recognized as such and receiving direct communications. Customers very much want to feel that suppliers know they are dealing with loyal consumers. They have only to squeak for the supplier to stand to attention. Their purchasing patterns are known and rewarded. They are important to the supplier, and the supplier makes the customers aware of their value. Thus are long-standing relationships established.

In the new marketing era, all such personally adapted communication can be generated without personal intervention—indeed, in some cases it is even preferable to generate these relationships without personal intervention. An assistant in a fashion store may very well recognize a client's face after half a year, but will not instantly remember the client's measurements and tastes. A database, on the other hand, has no problem whatsoever retaining these facts or other information about the customer's average expenditure, quality standards, or preferred brand. We won't even mention the fact that the employee who served the customer the last time has moved on to a different job and been replaced.

Though it may seem contradictory that personal relationships can be developed without personal intervention, the development of information and media means that this can be achieved with considerable success. And this is what increasingly keeps the commercial process afloat, in a society with an incomprehensible profusion of choices, with top-quality goods and services that are totally interchangeable, and with a decreasing socioeconomic security. It is customer relations that count, provided that all the other marketing factors are interchangeable. Nonetheless, in the last chapter we will see that actual personal contact can still be an important component.

NOTES

1. S. Rapp and T. Collins, *The Great Marketing Turnaround*, Prentice Hall, Englewood Cliffs, NJ, 1990; P. Postma, "Marketing Is Becoming a Different Profession," *Marketingstrategie & Verkoopkunde*, Harvard Classic, Borsen International Publications BV, Amsterdam and Brussels, 1989; P. Postma, "Interactive Marketing Creates a New Marketing Dynamic," *Holland Management Review*, No. 37, 1993, pp. 7–15.
2. E. J. McCarthy, *Basic Marketing: A Managerial Approach*, Richard D. Irwin, Homewood, IL, 1981.
3. J. C. Hoekstra, "Direct Marketing: van respons tot relatie" ("Direct Marketing: From Respondent to Relation"), inaugural speech, Erasmus University, Rotterdam, December 15, 1994.
4. G. Hallberg, *All Consumers Are Not Created Equal: The Differential Marketing Strategy for Brand Loyalty and Profits*, John Wiley & Sons, New York, 1995.
5. P. Postma. "De nieuwe marketingdynamiek" ("The New Dynamics of Marketing"), *Handboek Direct Marketing* (*Direct Marketing Handbook*), pp. A1100 and 1–23, Samsom, Alphen a/d Rijn, The Netherlands, 1994.
6. A. Fisherman, *The Guide to Mail Order Sales*, 1983.

THE INFORMATION REVOLUTION

This chapter examines exactly what is changing in the field of information technology, what main developments are taking place, and how these influence our perceptions and actions, specifically with regard to economic exchange: about buying and selling, about winning and retaining markets, and about market management. We won't discuss the world of information technology as such, but will look at it from the perspective of a marketer and manager to judge exactly what is changing in the world.

The following components offer a good starting point for understanding the information revolution.

- Digitalization
- Capacities
- Software
- Networks

EVERYTHING GOES DIGITAL

The first development that has changed the world is the ability to convert just about every sensory stimulus into zeros and ones: digitalization. Computer screens, with their visual representation of letters and numbers, are the most familiar application of digitalization. Graphics and tables are slightly more complex, but have also become standard formats. We can create, save, process and edit, send and receive, and print all sorts of documents.

Apple computers presented the most accessible interface, which was later duplicated by other computers such as the DOS machines with their Windows software. Thanks to compact disks, digital-quality sound has become the norm. Now that full-color motion pictures have also gone digital, and can be combined with everything else in the digital domain, the world can actually look very different. The next step to perfection is already on the horizon: three-dimensional visual reproduction techniques.

Our visual and aural senses are already being stimulated by impulses that can be wholly constructed within the digital domain. The ability to stimulate the senses of smell and taste is not yet as far advanced, but experiments are being carried out in these fields. Even simulating the sense of touch is no longer an impossibility. Digital construction in its most extreme involves the creation of *virtual reality*—an entirely digital environment into which a person can enter. The special data glove allows the subject to feel and weigh those things that are seen and heard. The manipulation of the senses is so convincing that the participant in this make-believe world perceives it as reality. Two people who are physically separated can communicate as if they were holding on to each other.

The consequences of the digitalization of everything that the human brain is capable of perceiving can be profound. For example, work can come to you rather than you having to travel to work. The same is true of education: It can be delivered on-line in a digital form, as can banking services, travel information, and every possible form of recreational activity. Many people believe that teleshopping will be an everyday reality in the near future. In fact, there's no need to leave the house; you can have everything delivered. A 24-hour economy will develop as a matter of course, since opening hours no longer have meaning. Rush hour may become a thing of the past. Work can be done at the time that suits the worker, and recreation time can be spread out across the whole week. Is a completely different society in the making?

This so-called digital society is described in depth by Nicholas Negroponte in *Being Digital*.[1] However picturesque his descriptions, they seem to overlook the importance of basic, analog, interpersonal communication and human motivation. From our point of view, it is precisely in combination with that world that digitalization becomes meaningful. We will return to this interrelationship in later sections of the book.

Some reservations about the new digital society are quite justifiable. For many jobs it is true that you no longer need to go to work, but that the work can be sent to you. Teleworking, still in its infancy, will definitely become more widespread. For those jobs that take place in an office with computers, teleworking is a logical step. But for a cook or a nurse, a dockworker or a waiter, it is an unlikely scenario. Teleworking will probably have its greatest impact, not in the reduction of traffic, but in the transfer of work from the West to those parts of the world where labor is considerably cheaper. If meetings or negotiations have to take place regularly, then we have to ask whether telephones, videoconferences, and videophones on their own will become satisfactory forms of communication. After all, people miss out on important aspects of dialogue that occur only in the realm of analog communication, as discussed in Chapter 4.

Even so, people who say that we will no longer need to leave the house in order to do our shopping too easily conclude that teleshopping will take off in a big way. We tend to forget that running a shop or warehouse is a professional occupation in its own right, and that goods have to be in stock, and be paid for, delivered and exchanged, and repaired or installed if necessary. Even more, going shopping is often just an excuse to get out of the house. Substantial amounts of money have already been spent on research in these areas. Those who argue for information technology (IT) are often so enthusiastic that they tend to deny the existence of any limitations and see all technical problems as ultimately surmountable. From the marketing viewpoint that forms the basis of this book, we will sometimes conclude differently.

Ultimately it all comes down to people and their irrational behavior.

IT-oriented people might argue that there is no longer any point in giving CDs as birthday presents, because the same combination of zeros and ones can be requested via a communication line. Because the music is no more than a specific binary sequence—which can in fact be sent to anybody at any given moment—a disk in a box is no longer necessary. As a marketer, you might ask yourself about the function of a CD. It can be a symbol of thoughtfulness, a token of thanks, or a present that caters to a specific taste, as expressed in a particular piece of music. In this case, there is also the pleasure of presenting a package wrapped in paper and a ribbon, something physical to hand over. A nice way of combining the technical possibilities with the physical presentation is to create a personalized CD. You could personally choose the digits that you would like on your CD and have the disk specially made for you. That the music is nothing more than a series of zeros and ones in a particular sequence is irrelevant. The box could just as well have contained chocolates. Thus many things can perform their primary function in a digital form, but this does not necessarily fulfill the functions of the article to be marketed.

It therefore remains to be seen to what extent these developments will turn into practical applications. Not everything that is possible is put into practice. And that which is functionally digitalizable does not necessarily have to be digital in order to be marketed. This is exactly the challenge that awaits the marketer in the new marketing era. It is not unbridled fantasy about what is technically possible; it is about trying to judge and forecast which of the technological possibilities will become part of everyday commercial reality. Marketing is certainly propelled by technology, but this technology merely provides us with possibilities; they do not have to be used. Some technologies were known for centuries before their main applications were discovered. Electricity was in use in the French court as early as the eighteenth century, but only for the amusement provided by electrifying chickens. That it could be used to provide light if it was dark outside didn't occur to anyone. In fact, many new inventions have their origins in entertainment. Centuries later, the same was true with the personal computer.

Digitalization has launched an important trend. More and more senses can be influenced with increasing refinement by impulses that are digitally constructed. The digital nature of the information means that it can be stored and manipulated relatively easily with computers, and sent anywhere where there is the capacity to receive it and the processing power to cope with it. This topic is discussed more fully below.

In all this, we must be careful not to ignore one complicating factor. Although we can indeed influence people in many ways with digital impulses, people are only human. In Chapter 4 we will examine the surprising consequences. Logically constructed search structures and choice patterns are not always applicable to humankind. *Nothing seems more unstructured and illogical than human behavior itself.* Further, we have to recognize and process everything with our senses, which have been determined by evolution and which have hardly changed for tens of thousand of years. That's why the CD will not immediately disappear, even if it is arguably technologically superfluous, because its physical existence has significance for us that reaches beyond the information it may contain.

UNLIMITED CAPACITIES

The conversion of everything into zeros and ones requires different sorts of capacity. In this section we will consider:

• Storage and transfer capacity
• Processing capacity
• Reduction of required capacity by data compression

Technically speaking, reduction of capacity is of a different nature but it leads to the same result—namely, an increased potential to perceive stimuli that are converted into binary language.

STORAGE AND TRANSFER CAPACITY

The *electronic superhighway* applies to the storage, distribution, and reception of binary information. The term is so graphic that it easily conveys a more concrete impression than is justified by what it describes. It was popularized by Vice President Al Gore, whose father was involved in the construction of the large railway networks in the United States; perhaps that played a role.

The electronic highway is made up of a large number of lines, cables, and connections that make it possible to receive data, sound, and images at home. The debate over which lines, cables, and connections should take priority has not yet been decided. In most Western countries, people already have two networks that reach into their living room: the telephone system and cable television. In fact, these two networks complement each other perfectly. The telephone network may be "narrow" in the sense that it is suitable for speech and data but not for moving pictures, but it has the advantage that people can address one another individually. It is basically a two-way network—the signals can go back and forth. In addition, its use can be measured and billed in terms of distance and duration. Internationally there is a high level of uniformity. There are some interesting solutions afoot to make "broad" use of the essentially "narrow" telephone lines.

The cable TV network is characteristically broad and allows the transmission of moving color pictures, but it is not designed for addressing people individually. What's more, the degree of penetration varies considerably in each country. In Belgium, about 92 percent of subscribers are reached per household, while France and the United Kingdom have a penetration of only 10 percent. In the United States the penetration of basic cable per TV household is 67 percent (as of 1998). Broadband signals can be sent from one central transmitter to all connected points. Basically it is a one-way network, but it can be adapted for return signals with the appropriate equipment. The measurement of usage per household was not taken into account during installation, but adaptations are being made.

The six major cable operators in the United States had a total of 66 million household subscribers in 1997. The subscriber growth is slowing, and huge investments are required to upgrade the systems and to install interactive capabilities.[2] Optical cables give the telephone network an enormous bandwidth; many of the main routes are already served by optical cable, but extending cable to everyone's front door will require considerable investment. Besides, there are all manner of technical developments that reduce the discrepancy in capacity and performance between one-way and two-way cables. As a result, one-way cable can be used for two-way traffic and broadband traffic can be transmitted through the old-fashioned, thin, copper cable.

But the electronic superhighway is not just about the cable and telephone network; it is also about radio and satellite connections. These too play a significant role in the influence of new media. The most remarkable phenomenon in this area is the mobile telephone. Whether in football grounds or conference rooms, people are glued to their telephones. In Italy, the mobile telephone has become so popular that the making of calls has been banned during church services. The mobile phone is a narrow form of communication in the sense that it is restricted to speech and data, but the advantages of no longer having to be connected to a wire is so significant that this limitation has done little to reduce its overwhelming popularity. The European standard for the Global System for Mobile Communications (GSM) covers more than 70 countries including the United States and Canada with a total population of more than a billion people.* The wireless, two-way communication of digital information means that it can be sent and received anywhere in the world: Faxes can be sent and received and agendas can be updated no matter where you are. The first attempts to commercialize the so-called personal digital assistants have been unsuccessful, but that does-

---

*Use of the GSM standard in North America indicates that GSM now plays a dominant role in the digital wireless landscape. It is not known which wireless communications technologies will become dominant in North America in years to come.

n't detract from the fact that mobile data traffic will show an explosive growth. A watch that can receive messages is on the market.

This whole field of development is characterized not only by its explosive rate of development, but also by an increasing pluralism that can easily appear chaotic. Certainly the consumer will have difficulty keeping abreast of these developments. They are already starting to cloud the careful definitions we gave earlier for the telephone and cable TV systems. If you use the Internet for phone calls, you don't pay per unit. Conversely, with digital decoders, the principle of unit payment is applied to the cable network in the form of pay-per-view. We have to wonder whether those countries with the most extensive cable networks are actually at an advantage in the development of electronic services. A high percentage of cable users could indeed be a disadvantage in the move toward direct-to-home transmission through your own satellite dish that picks up the footprint of a transponder. This direct-broadcast satellite (DBS) beams TV content and data from a satellite directly to any TV via a dish. Some DBS companies offer dozens of channels for very competitive prices. The law of the restricting lead could very well pertain to those countries that are the farthest in applying optical fiber technology.

For all these reasons, it becomes difficult to describe the various technical possibilities in simplified terms. And we have not even touched on the complex issues such as the conflicting interests, objectives, and influence of the companies in these market segments that compete in a life-and-death struggle while cooperating closely in other segments. Those who can deal with chaos will be the victors on this battlefield.

A key issue here is the infrastructure's capacity for storage and transfer of data. Expansion means increased capabilities; but as with other technological developments, how and when these advances will be achieved remains to be seen. Still, the enormous and multifaceted growth of these storage and transfer capabilities means that the seemingly self-evident limitations will suddenly disappear. Thus completely different options emerge.

PROCESSING CAPACITY

Something perhaps even more impressive is the speed with which microprocessors are developing. When Intel invented the microprocessor in 1971, 2300 transistors could be fitted on one chip using the existing printed line thickness of 6.5 μm. The thickness of the lines now is 0.5 μm, and the chip manufacturers can fit 35 million transistors on a single chip. *A standard 486 PC contains around 100 million transistors. And they cost a lot less than you would have to pay for 100 million sheets of toilet paper.*

The speed with which chips are being developed continues relentlessly. Technicians place no limit on this development, so you can use these figures to sketch what the future holds. The density of transistors on chips has roughly doubled every 18 months. If the pace indeed continues at the same rate, it could have an enormous impact on our daily lives. Here again we see that the opportunity for change and new applications depends entirely on the users and whether they actually want these changes. But they do seem to want them, considering the number of microprocessors that we already use in everyday items such as our ovens and cars. The E-type Mercedes introduced in 1995 incorporates 31 microprocessors in the fully equipped model, not counting the automatic windscreen wipers that begin to work when it starts to rain; that is an optional extra.

REDUCING CAPACITY BY DATA COMPRESSION

If the above discussion does not already offer enough possibilities for the future, there are also those techniques that drastically reduce the zeros and ones which have to be transferred and processed. This is called *data compression*. The abbreviation MPEG (followed by a number) stands for a compression system specifically for moving images.

You can see data compression at work in videoconferencing when the picture changes quickly. With the current ISDN-2 lines, the movements look jerky. Through data compression, only those parts of the picture that move are transmitted afresh; the rest are retained as is. In videotelephony, where pictures are sent across lines that are not designed to deal with images, this technique can also produce acceptable results.

In activities that are being undertaken to distribute interactive services on the cable networks, which include the possibility of ordering videos, these videos are compressed before transmission. This results in a considerable reduction of the time required to transmit a video of one and a half hours. The degree of data reduction largely depends on the type of picture, but averages a ratio of 1 to 40. That means that only 2.5 percent of the original number of bits and bytes are required.

All told, it can be concluded that technical developments create a scenario in which the capacity for storage, transfer, and processing of digital data is practically limitless. Thus for marketing applications there will no longer be any restrictions for practical use.

SELF-EXPLANATORY SOFTWARE

In addition to the digitalization of everything our senses are capable of perceiving and the development of endless capacity for storage, processing, and transfer, a third development plays an essential and defining role in the far-reaching changes in the world around us. That is the way people can work with the possibilities offered them by machines. When we step into a new car, we do not have to consult the instruction manual first in order to know what we use to steer and accelerate. More and more household gadgets are made so that people automatically use them correctly. *The equipment has to do what you think it will do, if you are to use it in the way you think you should use it.* That seems to be a simple and obvious statement, but in practice it is less straightforward. Marketers who have learned to use the media in the ways described in Chapter 1 know how they must structure a dialogue—printed or over the telephone—and design advertisements in order to get the consumer to react as intended. Clients or prospects have to follow the prescribed path while paying as little attention as possible to what they are doing. This is perhaps the most critical of the four aspects of the information revolution.

A solution for this problem is being sought in a number of ways. For example, there are three-dimensional representations of shopping streets or plazas, where you can choose the shop you like and go in—in other words, exactly what happens in the "real" world. But it looks as if this method of getting people to use a machine is unsuccessful. When people use a screen, they want to go straight to the intended destination and not have to encounter all the problems of finding the right shop, as they do in the real world.

One variation of this is a revolving carousel with text and symbols indicating what can be found in each compartment. An example is a carousel made in 1995 by Time Warner for its applications in Orlando. The carousel turns so that one of the choices appears directly in front of the viewer. The choices that are about to appear and those that have just gone past are also in the field of vision, but are somewhat less distinct. This seems to be a reasonable approximation of the natural field of vision experienced by people moving along under their own steam. The Ahold concern, with retail chains in the United States and Europe, has developed a teleshopping application with a similar carousel.

A second possibility for solving the problem of the machine/human interface is a cartoonlike figure that searches on behalf of the user. An old example of this is Microsoft's "Bob" in combination with a three-dimensional representation of Bob's house. The house consists of different rooms, each with furniture and other objects that represent a specific task or application, similar to Windows pictograms. The user is welcomed and shown around by the dog Rover, whose cartoon bubbles tell us what these objects do. There are 12 cartoon characters in the program, representing different levels of guidance. As often happens, the capacity required by the software is greater than that found in most PCs. Experience shows that the consumer does not respond particularly well to these types of figures.

Intelligent "agents" are a variation on the same principle.

The user gives the agent a task and it then goes in search of the desired application: service, supplier, or information. Agents can be found on the Internet in the form of advanced search systems. It is software that can be seen as a smart assistant with a large degree of independence that assesses all the information and possibilities and makes the correct choices, where necessary summarizing and/or presenting it. To imagine the Internet today without such agents is impossible. If you are a service provider on the Net, it is important to determine which agents select your services against which criteria.

A third approach is a straightforward menu—for example, represented as a number of boxes, each containing text or an image that indicates what the choice is. The problem here is that the information block has to indicate clearly what lays behind it. Would a pizza home-delivery service be found under "services," "shopping," or "food"? With the provider that I tried, it turned out to be under "services," after I had already searched extensively under "food" and then "shopping." For other services there can be little misunderstanding—for example with "videos" or "news." A curious choice is "various" or "other." Nobody can imagine what this means, except the service providers themselves.

With teleshopping services, straightforward pages with a selection of articles—as in a mail-order catalog—are making a comeback; the user can "zoom in" on articles of interest.

Hardware is also a subject of interest to ergonomics experts. The mouse that moves the cursor across the screen is being developed further. The Massachusetts Institute of Technology (MIT) in Boston has developed a mouse whereby objects on the screen are given weight and volume, in some ways comparable to the virtual reality glove, although here it produces only counterpressure. A mouse without a cable is also now possible.

The ideal solution has not yet been discovered, but extensive professional research is being carried out that will lead to solutions where people can utilize the technological possibilities more or less intuitively and without an instruction manual at hand. In this way the use of information technology becomes accessible to the general public.

NETWORKS

The final aspect of the information revolution that we will consider is the rise of networks. In order to judge their significance for the new marketing era, it is a good idea to mention a few basic concepts that can be considered forerunners to networks.

The difference between on- and off-line is one with which we are familiar. When on-line, the user is connected to either a central or a noncentral source, a database. Off-line means there is no other connection than with the data on the user's own medium. On-line can be unidirectional—from the source to the user—but there can also be two-way communication. These differences are important for the level of interactivity, a concept that we will return to in more detail in the next chapter.

A personal computer can be such a rich source of information, with such a wide range of choices, that there is already an enormous amount of interaction between the medium and the user, even without a connection to an outside source of information. But in this case the user is restricted to the medium or information carrier that exists in house. An example is a CD-ROM that is not connected to another source through a modem. Off-line is a different form of interactivity from on-line, two-way communication.

The next possibility is an on-line, two-way connection, not just between a single user and a source, but between various users and sources that are all interconnected. If the users and sources are local, the connectivity is a *local area network* (LAN); if they are geographically more widespread, it is a *wide area network* (WAN). These systems are often used for company computers with restricted access and are called Intranets. Finally, there is the Internet itself, with millions of sources ("servers") and tens of millions of users around the world. If the communications on a network consist of a combination of data, video, and sound, then it is obvious that something new is afoot. Multimedia PCs, which can deal with data, image, and sound, have become standard issue with the arrival of the Pentium chip.

Alongside the Internet, a completely open system that no

single person owns or controls and that anybody can set up a service in and take a look around, there are networks organized by owners that charge a fee. In the United States, and more recently in Europe, these include America Online©, CompuServe©, and Prodigy©. CompuServe© in particular is active on a global scale. These electronic information services also offer all sorts of transactional possibilities plus access to the Internet. In addition, there are "digital cities"—for example, Amsterdam and West Hollywood—consisting of a network of users and service providers.

Software companies are bringing their own electronic on-line networks onto the market. For example, Microsoft has introduced the commercial network service Microsoft Network (MSN) with the Windows 95 operating system. Users can connect directly to the network from within Windows, so it is particularly user-friendly.

Videoconferencing and video-on-demand are also network services. The terminology relating to networking is not used uniformly. Novum, a British research company, has studied the network markets in Europe and the United States up to the year 2000, and differentiates between:

- Conferencing systems (installations for videoconferences)
- Office computers (multimedia applications in the business market—for example, desktop videoconferences)
- Consumer products (primarily with news services tailored to the consumer).

Intense growth is expected in these last two sectors.

Our senses are manipulated more and more efficiently with digital stimuli; storage, transfer, and processing capacities are expanding explosively; and software has become increasingly accessible to a broader public. The end result is that, as sufficiently powerful computers connect to networks, a new dimension to communication and therefore to marketing is emerging. Perhaps we should assume that the first three key points fulfill their real potential only when they are accessed via a multimedia PC in local and global networks.

THE VALUE OF INFORMATION

Up to now we have discussed the information revolution only in terms of its technical components and its consequences for commercial processes. But that is only one aspect of the revolution. Also crucial is the content of the information—the meaning of the zeros and ones, the bits and bytes. The quantity of information available has mushroomed into a colossal mass. But what can we do with it in business transactions? If we want to avoid providing information, perhaps we should supply far too much, so that the relevant information is overlooked. This section examines the value of information in the framework of the information revolution, the commercial use of databases, and the role of information in the new marketing era.

THE LESS INFORMATION, THE BETTER

How much information can someone absorb at one time? Naturally, this depends on all sorts of factors, but a few examples from daily life will reveal the limitations. If you take the stairs to the fourth floor of a building, and there are two flights of stairs for each floor, you will notice that you begin to lose count between the second and third floors—that is, somewhere between five and six flights. The same happens when swimming lengths of a pool or listing colors. By the fifth to seventh category, many people will start to wonder whether they have already mentioned a certain category.

The quantities that a person can recognize in one glance certainly do not extend into multiples of ten. In fact, a human doesn't get much further than a duck. If a duck has four eggs and you take one away, then she will carry on brooding undisturbed. But if she has three eggs and you take yet another away, she immediately notices the difference and her brooding will be disturbed. *A duck can count to three, but a person doesn't get very much further.* Our short-term memory goes only to seven. This is an important warning for working with information. If people have to make a decision on the basis of a number of figures presented to them, they are very unlikely to be able to take 10 or so variables into consideration.

This means that the urge to collect as much information as possible is certainly not always the best way to make good decisions. Imagine someone making a decision on the basis of four or five figures from a random collection of a hundred. The person can easily choose a couple of figures from that hundred that lead to a totally incorrect decision. The more information, the more arbitrary it can be. Therefore, the issue is not amassing lots of information, but rather distilling from the whole mass of available data the information that has the greatest predictable value. With the possibility of accessing such enormous quantities of data in the workplace or from a central databank, the vital question becomes which data can produce the most useful information. The ease of storing data is a significant risk: Before you know it, you cannot see the forest for the trees. Meanwhile many tools have been developed to help distill the correct information from data, a process often referred to as *data mining*. Tools to find relevant information might include a simple gains chart; various statistical techniques, such as regressional analysis and multiple correlation calculations, as well as neural networks and genetic algorithms can also be useful.

FAMILIAR APPLICATIONS

Market research and marketing have long been interwoven. The discovery of such a discipline as marketing policy is closely tied to the existence of the phenomenon of market research. Plenty of research is still being conducted on market size, preferences, opinions, areas of interest, reading and viewing behavior, property acquisition, and premeditated purchases. All inquiries are intended to assist in the execution of a profitable marketing policy.

Market research is divided into qualitative and quantitative. Qualitative research, which sometimes precedes quantitative research, defines the themes or problem areas surrounding the subject being researched. Although the research cannot quantify just how many people hold a certain opinion and to what degree, it can discover the most widely held opinions about, for example, the way a company operates. On the basis of the supposedly relevant subjects uncovered, accurate questions can be formulated for quantitative research. In this way, statistics can be obtained about who agrees or disagrees with a point suggested by qualitative research. If sufficiently large quantities are chosen, conclusions can be reached that have a reasonable statistical probability of representing the population as a whole. But be careful. It is all about what people say they think, read, own, or buy.

Market information can also be collated from desk research, from existing data collected by government bodies or sectors within an industry, or from other sources of previous research. This type of statistical information might be based on real figures for production, consumption, export, and so forth. However, the figures are known only on an aggregated level.

All these forms of market research will continue to have their place, and superficially it seems as if not much has changed. However, there are two crucial differences regarding the impact of the information revolution and of the media revolution (described in the next chapter). First, the traditional forms of qualitative and quantitative market research are predominantly based on information provided by interviews and questionnaires. People are telephoned and asked about what newspapers they read; travelers are stopped in airports and asked how many times they fly each year; families receive questionnaires at home which they are asked to complete. The information is therefore based on people's responses to questioning. As indicated in Chapter 1, there can be a considerable difference between the answers given and actual behavior. Second, there is regular statistical information on production, consumption, and so on, but it is not available to an individual within a company or a household. The technical components of the information revolution, in tandem with the associated media revolution, now make it increasingly possible to manage markets according to actual behavior on an individual level. From our experience we can state that a completely different picture of the market will often emerge, with all the consequences for marketing policy that this holds. How can the market information from the old marketing era be so deceptive?

INFORMATION CAN BE DECEPTIVE

There are various reasons that information based on what people claim can be deceptive. Behavioral psychologists have explored this subject in countless publications, which are very useful for marketing. For now, however, we will limit ourselves to phenomena that are widely familiar. In Chapter 4, we will return to the association between behavioral psychology, neurology, and commerce.

The first indication of a disparity between reported behavior collected by market research and actual behavior surfaces when in retrospect the results "don't seem to be correct." This is often the case with election results, when, despite all the polls, the actual results come as a total surprise. The discrepancy is not that "the research is all wrong," because it has probably been conducted perfectly correctly. Rather, people said they did one thing to the researchers and did something entirely different in the polling booth. The research is correct, but the value of the resulting information for forecasting is negligible. To minimize these differences, researchers have asked people how they voted as they are leaving the polling station. One can hardly get any closer to the actual behavior. But even here marked differences with reality can result.

Market research carried out by a leading women's organization in the 1950s, just prior to the opening of self-service shops, showed that 90 percent of housewives would never do their shopping in such a store. All sorts of reasons were given, all of them plausible: the desire to chat with the shop assistant, the ease of handing over a shopping list, and the concern about buying too much. In reality, however, the exact opposite proved true: Self-service stores were a great success. Now it is almost impossible to shop any other way.

More than 30 years later, market research by banks in the Netherlands about automatic teller or cash machines (ATMs) had exactly the same result. It showed that at the most the better-educated customers might occasionally make use of a cash dispenser. But the banks shouldn't pin too much hope on the new service. The research was important to determine how quickly the ATMs needed to be installed. Once again reality proved to be diametrically opposite to the results obtained by market research.

In situations with which people are unfamiliar, questions about intent clearly have no value for establishing what will actually happen. Market research into intended use of new media is therefore equally nonsensical. We apparently cannot give relevant answer to questions that relate to situations with which we are not intimately familiar. Nonetheless, research of this type continues to be performed regularly. Research carried out by the Trendbox bureau into new media brought to light that the worst-scoring new medium in terms of familiarity and use was the voice-response telephone—namely, the telephone call that is handled by a computer which gives information in response to the caller tapping in or dialing numbers. But if we look at the real situation, it is abundantly clear that this is by far the most frequently used new medium, used much more often than the CD-i (CD-interactive), which scored much better in the research but collapsed shortly after.[3] Whatever purpose this kind of research serves, it does not serve to give some indication of future use.

Even in situations where people are familiar with the subject in question, those interviewed can structurally give incorrect answers. On daytrips for housewives organized by Wehkamp, the Netherlands' foremost mail-order company, the participants were asked at the beginning and end of the guided tour whether they ever bought anything from Wehkamp. Statistically speaking, Wehkamp could easily predict by using its database what percentage of the women present should put up their hands. At the beginning of the excursion, only between a quarter to a third of the average number who must have been customers put up their hands. The rest lied. It was only after the excursion that the number of hands in the air tallied with the percentages that Wehkamp knew to be correct. Bruynzeel is a leading brand of kitchens in a number of European countries. When consumer research was held in these countries, the market share for Bruynzeel always appeared much higher than Bruynzeel knew it to be from the number of units produced. Apparently when asked about the make of their kitchen fittings, people say "Bruynzeel" without knowing the actual brand. The same is true of subscribers to daily and weekly newspapers. We will not discuss why the facts differ from the answers given, but simply underline how unreliable information about reported behavior can be.

In the examples given so far, no mention has been made of selective perception or of the fact that it can be in someone's interests to misrepresent the facts. If this is actually the case, it only makes matters worse.

Selective perception is the phenomenon by which people recognize far faster things they know than things they have not yet been confronted with. If you are about to change jobs, and you have an interview with Ernst & Young, you will suddenly notice just how many Ernst & Young offices there are. The offices were there the week before; it is just that you didn't notice them. If you develop an interest in a certain model of car, you will suddenly see this car everywhere. "Aren't there a lot of convertibles?" will be your surprised reaction once you have decided that you would like to buy a convertible. It is not that there are suddenly more convertibles than there were previously. If people were asked how many convertibles they see each day, their answer would depend, not so much on the number of convertibles that actually drive past, but rather on whether their attention had been attracted by them. Preconceived images build recognition. We will return to these types of phenomena in Chapter 4.

On the other hand, people hardly remember the things they know well but have never paid special attention to. If a building is demolished on a road that you use every day, you would struggle to picture it, even though you thought you could see every building in your sleep.

Moreover, perceptions depend heavily on mood or attitude. If you ask two sales representatives about the opportunities in a certain market, one may see chances everywhere, while the other sees none. Yet they are both referring to the same market. The answer therefore depends not so much on the market as on who's answering the question. Such questions do not provide information about the market but about those being questioned. If there is a vested interest at play, then the information becomes completely untrustworthy. If people earn a percentage on the basis of their forecast, then they quite rightly avoid being too optimistic in their estimate. But if people stand to gain something by making an optimistic forecast, and a plausible excuse is always at hand to justify the actual outcome, or the actual realization of these forecasts is not so important within the company, then the forecasts for that same product in the very same market are bound to be higher.

In one of my first jobs I was responsible for the sale of mobile storage systems. We were able to sell these systems very successfully throughout Europe, as well as in the Middle East. There was one exception, however, and that was in one sales area of Holland. The representative was convinced that his clients had no interest in mobile systems, and proved that with his results: Hardly any mobile systems were sold in his area. With my limited experience I saw no reason to question the insight of such an experienced salesperson. That was until another sales representative took over that same area. He was unaware of this tale, and simply went out and sold storage systems. Once again it was a case, not of the market, but of the individual.

If personal esteem is at issue, then the reality as experienced seems remarkably often to favor somebody's own merit. Salespeople will often give themselves the credit for closing a sale but will rarely accept the blame for losing a deal. In the latter case, it is usually a result of factors beyond their control. Similarly, anything that proves us right is something we perceive with unusual ease. Discussions between two competitors are all too easily seen as a victory for the party who is expressing the views that the supporter shares. Forecasts for football results are remarkably in favor of the clubs that people support. *The forecast says less about the result than about the person making it.*

Last of all, memory is totally unreliable when people are under emotional strain. People who have been victims of highly emotional events can give what they think is an honest account of what happened, but it is by no means certain that this is what actually happened. According to the evidence of the black box retrieved from the El-Al jumbo jet that crashed in the Bijlmermeer near Amsterdam in 1992, the airplane made its approach from quite the opposite direction to that initially deduced from eyewitness statements. Survivors of the Martinair crash in Faro, Portugal one year later, said that the aircraft had attempted to land on up to three separate occasions. The black box showed that the aircraft crashed on its first attempt to land.

We have to conclude that what people say about what they see, about their buying patterns, and about their intended behavior says little about what they actually see, buy, or do. People's statements have more to do with ideas formed in their heads on the basis of knowledge, individual history, and mood. *If you want to learn about the ins and outs of a market, do not listen to what the clients say. Instead, find out what they do.*

USING MARKETING DATABASES

Given the enormous development in capacity and processing power, given the software developments and the increasing use of networks as described in the first half of this chapter, and given the increasing importance of information in every possible process, it looks as if information will become increasingly important in the management of the commercial process. Because of the wealth of information available to us, we have to consider which information is actually useful. The increasing accessibility of databases and software makes it easier to find out what information is valuable for forecasting—and what is not.

In the new marketing era, the information revolution acquires an excellent form in marketing databases. Marketing databases replace the market research reports from the old marketing era, but without taking over the old form completely. At the moment, databases are being created in many businesses, but understandably they are often used in traditional ways. A new phenomenon is frequently still translated in traditional ways. This is normal when a new trend generates structural changes. The first automobile was a carriage *without* a horse, but wasn't constructed or used much differently from a carriage *with* a horse. Many marketing databases are still used in the same way as market research tools and with traditionally formulated target groups. To clarify the various uses, we will examine three forms that we meet in practice: normal use, upside-down use, and use in the new marketing era.

NORMAL USE

Normal use of a marketing database is characterized by the performance of operational tasks in the same way they were carried out prior to the use of a marketing database. The database is generally introduced in a company during an automation project. Often it is part of a larger automation project, which must take into account a number of different functions within the company. It is initiated by automation needs and not by commercial or marketing considerations. These departments may well be involved as "users" that, according to the traditional automation approach, will have to specify their exact requirements.

The question is whether users are able to do that. Usually they refer to the present situation and try to indicate what information they want, how frequently and with what degree of accuracy: sales per product, per rep, per region, margin, etc. They can include operational functions such as telemarketing and generating mailing lists. But it is very doubtful whether the marketers can specify which information they require with the precision called for by automation. The trick within this sea of possibilities will be the ability to trace the relevant information. That is precisely the choice that must evolve when using the database once it has been completed. Moreover, this information is not static; it can change continually.[4]

Thus the marketing database for normal use is a typical automation project. The specified data will be accurately translated into a model, and lots of work will be done to input and connect the data to the production schedule, logistics, and administration. Once the system is operational, nobody will be able to function without it. This reliance incorrectly suggests that the project is a success. People can no longer do without it because they have made themselves dependent on the system, and thus it is a logical outcome of the project. The clients, activities, and products are carefully entered. Everybody has an unprecedented overview. But what else? Has the commercial function changed too? Are prospects with a higher likelihood of making purchases recognized as such and handled differently from other prospects? Or does everybody simply do the same as before, but do it a lot easier thanks to the automated systems?

When a company wants to send off a mailing, a little box is ticked for the relevant clients. But *why* a box has been ticked is something the database cannot explain or justify. It is actually a marketing manager's decision reached on the basis of knowledge, as described earlier.

How deceptive these sorts of judgments can be was once again shown by one of my company's clients, who contacted the company because "so many things still went wrong with the marketing database, and the anticipated results were not achieved." In a mail shot, 80 percent of the mailings were correctly selected according to the selection criteria given by the marketing manager. But the remaining 20 percent seemed mistakenly to consist of those very prospects who should not have been included because they did not satisfy any of the selected criteria. Apparently this was seen as an operational issue. The client presented it to us as an illustration of how much still went wrong with database-managed marketing. Sure, that was also true, but the real problem was overlooked. The 80 percent "correctly" mailed prospects achieved a conversion rate of 5.9 percent. Nobody had even looked at the conversion of the remaining 20 percent—after all, hadn't they gone wrong? But when we asked for the rate to be calculated, the result was also exactly 5.9 percent. If a random mailing had been organized using this database, the result would also have been 5.9 percent. The conclusion to be drawn from this mess-up was that the marketing manager's selection criteria contributed absolutely nothing to improving the result.

Whether the prospects satisfied the criteria made no difference to the result. Thus, people went to a lot of trouble to no effect, and did not even notice it. By analyzing the respondent results, we were able to improve the selection criteria to such an extent that a result of 10 percent was achieved, with the same number of mailings.

The new marketing era is still so new that many available software packages are unable to provide an adequate answer. Operational functions can usually be carried out without any problem, but the intelligent commercial management functions are only rarely found in such packages. The performance of operational functions can nevertheless be useful, specifically when the commercial function is performed with difficulty or in a chaotic way. An automation project can help create some order. People replace the traditional horse with a combustion engine, but the carriage and its function stay the same.

UPSIDE-DOWN USE

If normal use is neutral toward the information used, then the value of the information in *upside-down use* is actually negative. A marketing database offers the possibility of determining the reactions and transactions per name and address, thus creating the possibility of optimizing the investments in commercial activities. But strangely enough in practice we regularly see that people using the database score less well than if they had not made any selection at all. If the mistakenly and randomly mailed prospects in the previous example had achieved a score higher than 5.9 percent, this would have been such a case. Although the selection criteria probably contributed nothing, they didn't adversely affect the result either. They did, however, limit the market sector that was targeted, and incurred extra costs, so in that sense there was some sort of an upside-down use.

The essence of upside-down use is that you talk to the database instead of listening to it. In a traditional market approach, people have all sorts of ideas about the target group, or they think up some obvious target group for a certain product. Without a marketing database, people are able to approach this target group only as a generic whole, by choosing the correct advertising medium and tailoring the creative ideas to the prescribed target group. This upside-down use of the database doesn't change the process of target group determination. But people are able to make the target more precise by approaching individually by name and address those people who, according to data in the database, satisfy the prescribed criteria. Nevertheless, it is still not certain whether these criteria in themselves increase the chance of response or conversion into a sale. Personal prejudices are imposed on the database unchecked, whereby these biases are actually emphasized.

For example, when a target group is chosen, it is all too often that of younger, better-educated men and women with above-average incomes. It seems as if every marketing manager targets this group, and as if more products are directed at it than there are members of the group! Again, this probably has more to do with self-projection and other factors mentioned earlier than with the market.

One example of the upside-down use of databases leading to a worse result than if absolutely no selection had been made was provided by a client in the financial sector. The company had developed a capital investment product that, according to the marketing manager, was solely intended for those in the absolute top bracket of the company's database. The results were very disappointing, and so the company rented lists from third parties with names and addresses of people who were not yet clients. The outcome was considerably worse than with the first campaign. This was once again caused by an incorrect judgment—namely, that only the very well-to-do would be interested in the product. The reality was that those well-heeled individuals already had countless other methods of investing their wealth. When the product was offered as a test to a random sample of clients, the result was somewhat better. Next, the results of the test were analyzed using the characteristics already specified in the database, and with this information very satisfying results could be achieved. The selection criteria that actually seemed to work related not simply to wealth, but rather to the relationship the client had already established with the financial institution, assessed by the number of transactions and the duration of the relationship. The cost per $100,000 of invested capital in the first campaign with the very wealthy was around $100, while the costs for renting third-party lists ran to many hundreds of dollars. With the random tests the costs were well below $100 for very $100,000 of invested capital, and with the actual target group from the analysis the costs could be reduced to just $30.

Thus, if traditional marketing thinking is applied to a marketing database, the consequences can be damaging. Seemingly logical target groups seldom turn out to be the ones that offer an above-average chance of selling the product. In our experience of database marketing, we rarely find that the predetermined target group is in fact the correct one. The farther removed we are from the market, the greater the chance of a flop. For industrial businesses, with a small number of clients concentrated in specific sectors, the differences are much smaller than in consumer markets, where, thanks to the results of market research, people pretend to have an excellent idea of their customers. Often they can describe them in detail, but if you then say, "Just give me a list with the names and addresses of your best customers," they will be dumbstruck. Here lies the difference between the old and new marketing eras, best summarized in the adage: "The product was a success, but not with the target group." Clearly that was not the target group, but the thinking behind this principle is often so sacred that people simply do not realize it.

CORRECT USE IN THE NEW MARKETING ERA

Whoever dares to *listen* to the database instead of continually *talking* to it, and then dares to accept that the reality can be different from what was expected, can significantly improve the commercial results in most product/market combinations. To a large extent, this is a psychological problem. Commercial people in many companies are often said to "know the market." If a marketing database shows that the market is actually put together in a different way, this information is not always received with open arms. It is difficult to accept that we are wrong, and only a database that shows we are right can be considered any good.

One client had the firm conviction that the customers consisted primarily of 20- to 40-year-olds, the constantly used criterion. Because I did not believe this, a campaign was created so that we could distinguish between the results with people ages 20 to 40 and those with a group selected randomly from the database. The results of the first group did indeed seem better than those for the second, randomly chosen group. From our experience I could not understand the results, so at my request a test was carried out with a group ages 0 to 100 and a random group. The first group again scored better than the second, and scored the same as the first group in the earlier sales campaign. Further analysis brought to light that the age of approximately half the names in the database was known, while the other half was unknown. So it was not a matter of age, but rather whether the people involved had indicated their ages. Some of the people in the database had provided their telephone number. In a following campaign, when the criterion "telephone known/unknown" was used, the people for which the number was known scored somewhat better than the group for which the number was unknown. As it turned out, cross-referencing "telephone number known" with "age known" produced the most favorable result. Clearly, in this database, the information was an indication of the loyalty that the person felt toward the company, and the better this relationship, the better the response and conversion into sales.

Whoever listens carefully to the database will make the most unusual discoveries. The fact that the level of income often says little about the likelihood of purchase, even for more expensive products, is no longer a surprise. But some people still find it surprising that whether or not a certain address features a garden says nothing about the chance of someone buying flower bulbs or garden furniture. As we saw in Chapter 1, this is simply a matter of fact.

A bank made a clear distinction among its level of clients. The top clients were reasonably spoiled, but those at the lowest end of the scale were regarded as nuisances who cost more than they yielded. The bank considered this group "no-good clients." On closer inspection, it turned out that a not insignificant number within this group lived in the same postal district as the top clients. They seemed like clients who would be very attractive for the bank. What's more, the bank already had some relationship with them, even though it was minimal. Obviously, these people regarded the bank in question as a "no-good bank" and did their serious banking elsewhere. The bank could make just as much return on investment with this group of "lower-ranking" clients as with its top clients.

"Measure and ye shall know" is a well-known maxim that applies to using a marketing database according to the methods appropriate to the new marketing era. But this is not as simple in practice as it might appear. "Measure and ye shall know, and also sweat" is nearer the truth. If you take another look at Figure 1-1, you'll notice that in the old situation, the company calls out to the market and, as an extension, also calls out to the database. The company bombards the market with communications. This is the upside-down approach. It is a remnant of the old marketing era. In the new approach, the company listens and reacts. The database is a vehicle, and it is now being used according to the principles of the new marketing era. We no longer calculate the market from within the company, but instead communicate, listen, and record. The database will teach us what the market has to say. We rely on the media that make one-to-one communication possible, old as well as new: mailings, call centers, and new media instead of thematic campaigns. In other words, the thematic advertising campaigns that were the model for the old marketing era have been replaced by database-managed call centers for the new marketing era—the telephone instead of the advertisement. It is a case no longer of whether the company is large enough to be able to attract more attention than the others, but whether it is responsive enough to react quickly and appropriately.

INFORMATION IN THE NEW MARKETING ERA

At the beginning of this chapter, we used four technical components to examine the extent to which information is changing our society and its commercial operations. More and more stimuli that we experience are digital, meaning that they can be reproduced irrespective of the time, place, or person concerned. Storage, transfer, and processing capacities no longer form a bottleneck. Software is becoming increasingly intelligible to the average person, and networks continually create new communication structures.

A number of remarks can be made about the value of the information itself. Too much information is easily as worthless as no information at all. People are limited in the amount of information they can absorb, and the answers given say extraordinarily little about actual behavior. The traditional applications of market research have enormous restrictions. The combination of information technology and marketing information come together in the shape of a marketing database. But as so often happens with radical change in society, we apply traditional thinking to a new development and thus do not realize the full potential of a marketing database. Sometimes it remains simply part of an operational automation project, while at other times the projection of old principles onto a new idea actually leads to negative results. Remember that it took a decade in the development of the automobile before people realized that you could protect the coachman from the elements by extending the roof of the vehicle right to the windscreen. Human beings cannot help extrapolating what they are familiar with, and can see the new dimension only much later. In the case of marketing databases, people have to learn to listen in order to discover how the market is actually constructed.

If we project the information revolution onto the use of information for commercial processes, we can distinguish two dimensions that clearly show its impact. The first dimension is development of information for the mass of (potential) clients, down to specific target groups, then down to incorporating postal codes, and finally down to the smallest imaginable level, the individual who can be traced by name and address. Thus it is the dimension that moves from generalization to the specific and identifiable.

The second dimension is the development of the type of information used. Initially this was primarily information derived from studies using a variety of sources. Generally it was a combination of research data, plus assessments made by experts, leading to a final conclusion. That conclusion could also include elements of personal interpretation on the part of the compilers. It could deal with trends in society, the changing character of ethnic groups, or perhaps changes in moral attitudes. For a manufacturer of, say, roofing tiles, it is rather difficult to attempt to establish a connection between such information and the market.

Market research has developed alongside such derivative information. As discussed earlier, the information from market research is primarily based on stated behavior, and we saw how misleading such information can be, despite all the techniques that are used in market research to prevent distortion. Research does show people's response to questions they are asked, but is applicable only in a limited number of situations. You could even wonder whether the official listening and viewing figures are not actually figures just showing whether the radio or television is switched on.

In the new marketing era, we are shifting from derivative and self-reported information to behavioral analysis. It is the indisputable reflection of human behavior, and whether people, when asked, admit to it or not is irrelevant. Information technology makes it possible to determine behavior, even at an individual level, and even in mass markets. This information is by far the most trustworthy when forecasting future behavior. Our experience with database marketing operations is supported by the way in which the human nervous system is constructed. We will return to this interesting phenomenon in detail in Chapter 4, which also addresses the enormous disparity between actual and self-reported behavior.

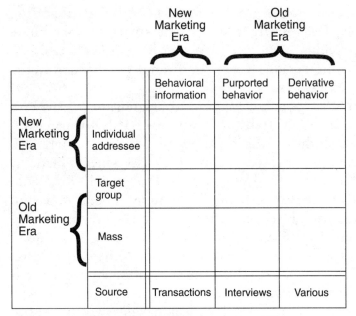

FIGURE 2-1.   The Marketing Information Matrix[R].

Both dimensions are illustrated in Figure 2-1. The old and new market eras are compared in terms of information. Behavioral information about individuals heralds the dawn of a totally new era in marketing.

NOTES

1. N. Negroponte, *Being Digital,* Knopf, New York, 1995.
2. Elizabeth Lesly, Ronald Grover, and Neil Gross, "Cable TV: A Crisis Looms," *Business Week,* October 14, 1996, pp. 100–106.
3. G. Eilander, "De consument over Nieuwe Media" ("The Consumer on New Media"), *Trendbox Report on Interactive Media,* part 2, presented at Media Workgroup Congress, Noordwijkerhout, The Netherlands, 1995.
4. Postma, Paul, *Het Direct Marketing Boek* (The Direct Marketing Book), Management Press, Amsterdam, 1990.

THE MEDIA REVOLUTION

A book is not the best medium to express the revolution taking place in the media. Developments are always a few steps ahead of what is written. For this reason, only the first section of this chapter discusses the rapidly advancing technical developments. The balance of the chapter offers a framework for reviewing the marketing implications of the media revolution. The precise state of media development at the time you read this book cannot be determined in advance. If you are up to date with the latest developments, you can pass over the opening section. But if all this terminology makes your head spin, read the introductory section fully so you can understand the consequences of these developments. Noticeably absent are descriptions of media tycoons, shifts in power and importance, mergers, and the like. They are not relevant in the context of this book, and can be followed by consulting the daily media.

The word *medium* is used differently by various professions. For our purposes, printed and electronic media are the information carriers in today's marketing world: newspapers, books, magazines, brochures, radio, television, and PCs. The telephone can also be included in this definition when interactive voice response is involved. Media are about the transfer of information without personal intervention. Telemarketing does not strictly satisfy these criteria. But because its structure involves a call center, it has many characteristics in common with media and deserves to be mentioned here.

Electronic media require a cable, CD-ROM, floppy disk, memory, network connection, and/or voice computer to communicate information via a screen and/or telephone. That's all there is to it. The carrier of the actual information—a CD-ROM disk, for example—is regarded by the computer industry as the information carrier, to differentiate it from the machine or hardware on which it is played and the software that drives it. These technical components are necessary to achieve the total effect. For our purposes, a medium refers to the whole array of hardware and software and information carriers.

GURUS MAKE MISTAKES

A classic work about media and their effect on society and the individual is *Understanding Media: The Extensions of Man,* by Marshall McLuhan.[1] Even though McLuhan lived until 1980, he did not consider the computer a medium. Nevertheless, computers did fall under his definition of media, which also included clothing, houses, money, cars—everything that influences our senses. Our definition of media is limited to their function in the marketing process. McLuhan was interested, not in the information carried by a medium, but in the social and psychological effects a medium has in extending our senses. That is how McLuhan's "the medium is the message" can be understood.

All the same, it is obvious that content is of decisive importance for the comprehension of a specific message, and that the medium that conveys the message can certainly play a part in how the message is perceived. It can hardly be claimed that it is only a question of the medium, independent of the content.

McLuhan's discussions of "electric media" come closest to the media that are the subject of this chapter. McLuhan expected that these media would cause a social and political implosion, "raising human awareness of responsibility to an intense degree." He thought that because these media, including television, made us aware of worldwide injustice, we would rise up against that injustice. I wish that were true. However, nothing in behavioral psychology predicts that an overexposure to abuse of human rights and the consequent disasters stimulates people to rise up and fight against it. A televised presentation of famine may create a short-lived incentive to make a donation, but structurally the growth of awareness about abuse has not led to growing streams of developmental aid and armies of people who selflessly fight against injustice. On the contrary, a barrage of displeasing images results in desensitization; we develop a filter that protects us.

In common with so many others, McLuhan allowed himself to believe that human behavior would improve if technology were more advanced. Similarly, Vice President Al Gore thought the electronic superhighway might mean better education and the revival of true democratic principles. Unfortunately, shortcomings in education or democracy have their roots in circumstances that will not be changed by the electronic highway. Nicholas Negroponte describes the changeover from the ancient atom to bits and bytes as if it were a liberation.[2] According to him, digital life is different, almost genetic in nature, in the sense that each generation is more digital than the last. Negroponte may not mean this literally, because the resulting rate of evolution would be equivalent to people losing their appendices in one generation. To conclude that the genes of a new generation significantly differ from those of the present is to believe, along with the French old farmer, that people breathe with their stomach. Since the dawn of evolution, we have possessed exactly the same characteristics and passions that drive us now. Not much will change by next week, or the next millennium. We therefore have to take as our starting point those constants of human behavior that the media can influence in the course of bringing about economic exchange. The possibilities are considerable.

The following section examines the key players in the media revolution. Again, the technical components serve as our framework for reviewing how the new media manage commercial processes, which conditions have to be satisfied, and what significant outcomes will result. The differences between the old marketing era and the new marketing era are also explored.

MEDIA CAN DO MORE AND MORE: THE TECHNIQUE

Let us begin by positing an ideal interactive supermedium (Figure 3-1). It is completely two-way in the sense that there is a connection to and from every point along which any transaction can be handled. It is multimedia in the sense that it involves data, sound, and moving film or video images.

Some existing media do come pretty close to this ideal. If we ignore for the moment the requirements of video pictures, then the supermedium is the telephone. Callers can contact each other with data and sound, and transactions can be made. If we consider the requirements for video with sound, then traditional television fulfills the ideal, except that communication is only one way. At best you can react in a limited way to TV, but you cannot make or transmit your own television programs for whoever wants to watch them. And as long as TV is not interactive, it is not a medium for handling transactions.

Let's turn instead to the multimedia PC with a connection to the Internet. Now here is a concept. You can indeed create a program for your PC and transmit it to the world. Your creation can include text, sound, and even live pictures of you, your surroundings, and anything else. With adequate security

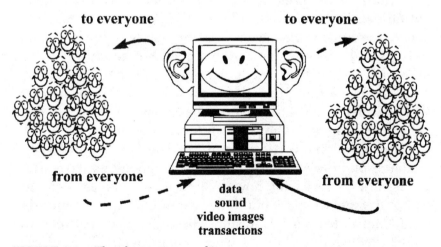

FIGURE 3-1.   The ultimate new medium.

measures you can also make transactions. Still, the quality is inferior to full-screen video. Jaded television viewers may think they are once again watching early TV transmissions. But progress is at hand: Second-generation hardware with screen-change algorithms produces 30 frames a second for full-screen video. The fascination is undeniable. We must conclude that the Internet PC comes pretty close to the ideal model.

The Internet is one of the fastest-growing media of all time. Research carried out on the Net itself indicates that around a third of the respondents work in computer-related sectors; a third of the European respondents and a quarter of the American respondents are involved in education. Other users include various professionals and managers. Users are generally prosperous, and their average age is increasing—from 31 years old in 1995 to around 40 years old in 1998. Favorite activities include surfing, playing games, collecting research material, and sending and receiving e-mail. Shopping is the least-mentioned reason for using the World Wide Web, but collecting information about commercial products and services is common.[3]

Up to now, at least one component has been missing from all our candidates for ultimate medium. Other criteria can also be listed—for example, suitability for accomplishing commercial processes—as discussed later in the chapter. Still, we have a benchmark. Two strands of development (though they are converging) summarize the most important technical components of the media revolution: developments stemming from the PC and those derived from TV.

DEVELOPMENTS BASED ON THE PC: MULTIMEDIA APPLICATIONS

Multimedia PC is a rather broad term for a PC with digital audio and a CD-ROM player. Sound can be communicated, and computer-animated moving pictures can be displayed. The "old" 486 PC is not designed for full-screen video. A multimedia PC with a modem allows information to be sent back and forth over the telephone lines.

In the computer industry, multimedia refers to the addition of moving pictures and sound capabilities to a computer's text and graphics capabilities. (In the advertising world, multimedia refers to a campaign that makes use of several forms of advertising media, such as newspapers, television, and billboards.) Most multimedia computer applications use Microsoft Windows software. In fact, the Windows concept has been a significant stimulus for multimedia PCs. The traditionally more user-friendly and multimedia-oriented Macintosh system from Apple can easily be integrated with the more widespread Windows system. As is often true—for example, with the standards for video movies—commercial superiority has nothing to do with technical superiority. A third combination of hardware and software that can serve as a platform for multimedia is CD-i. The OS/2 operating system from IBM can also form the basis for a multimedia PC; applications designed for Windows should run without any problem on an OS/2 computer.

CD-i and Apple Macintosh both conform to precisely defined standards; PCs are not quite so standardized. Thus converting a PC into a multimedia computer can be problematic. In an attempt to solve this problem, agreement has been reached on a standard configuration called MPC. If a PC conforms to this standard, then in principle upgrading should be no problem. With the reduction in prices, proliferation of choices, and difficulties of techware installation, nonexperts can just as well buy a new plug-and-play multimedia PC than upgrade an existing one.

CD, CD-ROM, DVD.   Some 40 percent of the annual Christmas sales of certain CD-ROMs in the United States and Canada are returned because of problems. If the consumer does succeed in installing the CD-ROM player, there can still be a flood of complaints, as detailed by a reporter from *The Wall Street Journal*. He bought *The Lion King* on CD-ROM for his son as a Christmas present. His front-page article about functional problems pulled no punches. Today, more than half the CD-ROMs—products originally designed for the professional market—are purchased by private individuals for domestic use. Such users encounter difficulties that they do not find with their televisions or videorecorders. Many of the more sophisticated titles will run only on fully equipped Pentium-based PCs. Nonetheless, these are only teething problems.

Figure 3-2 shows the forecast made by the Software Publishers Association (SPA) for CD-ROM consumer sales from 1995 to 1999. The projections are exceptionally high, but what are the facts? To start with, actual figures are very hard to come by, and different publications give different data. The $1 billion mark seems to have been reached in 1995—if not for the American market alone, then certainly for the world as a whole. (The figure is minute compared, say, with the sales of simple Nintendo games.) There seems to be no doubt that it is a fast-growing market, but the growth projections have been reduced to 30 percent from the earlier 50 percent. Further, the market is being glutted by CD-ROM producers. In 1998 alone, there are bound to be 10,000 or more new titles. The investment in a new title can amount to millions of dollars, so only a small percentage of the CD-ROMs released will break even. Obviously, an enormous shake-out will take place.

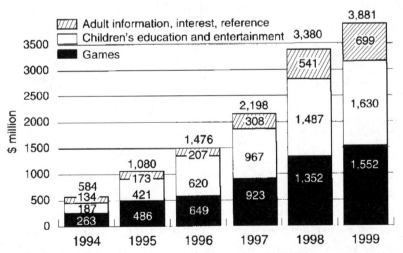

FIGURE 3-2.   Forecasted CD-ROM consumer sales from the Software Publishers Association (SPA) for IGGS. (Source: New Media Strategist, May 4, 1995.)

All in all, it is a buyer's market that has been completely overestimated, with too few consumers for a seemingly endless supply. So we need to be careful about predicting sales in the world of new media. Still, among the losers, a few winners will emerge. Games, entertainment, and edutainment continue to generate the largest turnover, because people do not tire of being amused. Yesterday's court jester has been replaced by the CD-ROM.[4]

The external source for a PC's data, sound, and pictures can be a floppy disk, a CD-ROM, or a telephone line with a modem. There are also possibilities for running CD-i's on a PC. Every system seems to be merging with every other system. Modems for connecting PCs to cable networks have an extremely high number of bits and bytes per second, and mean a further step in the direction of combining TV and PC technologies. With the commercialization of the high-density standard for CDs—the *digital versatile disc,* or DVD—the audio CD, CD-ROM, and CD-i can be grouped together. After all, the real multimedia machine will be born thanks to:

1. Convergence and compatibility.
2. Increasing capacities—from 74 minutes of sound for a CD to a full-length feature film for a DVD.
3. More flexibility. For example, a CD recorder can fill a CD only once, whereas a CD rewritable (CD-RW) can rewrite a CD 1000 to 10,000 times. And after the DVD-ROM player, we can expect the DVD recordable and DVD-RAM. The new generations of these machines will all be compatible, even with the new CD-ROM players with multiread functions.

Multimedia Notebooks.   Notebooks—portable, compact computers—illustrate the trend toward "small" and "anywhere you need it." Something that can work anywhere without a plug is more attractive than something that needs a connecting lead. Even without multimedia facilities, notebooks provide the mobility (much like mobile phones) that make them excellent sales support for traveling representatives.

Personal Digital Assistant.   The personal digital assistant (PDA) goes one step further. Fitted with an optical pen, this little tool enables you to write and draw on an electronic slate instead of typing away at a keyboard. A handwriting recognition program—part of the so-called Newton technology—translates the input into bits and bytes to be processed, sent, or printed. PDAs are actually little palmtop computers with extended agenda functions as well as memory cards and plug-in cards for special applications. Unlike notebooks, they do not have a port for disks, and there is still no sound or moving pictures. Still, the future has a lot to offer in this area.

DEVELOPMENTS BASED ON TV:
INCREASING INTERACTIVITY

Despite its relatively restricted visual communication, the PC gives the individual user the most extensive range of possibilities to execute the most varied instructions. By contrast, TV offers perfect audiovisual transmission but very limited choices. Users—often many simultaneously—can choose only from the possibilities offered. To be sure, the possibilities are growing as users opt for additional channels at higher subscription prices.

There is also the possibility of controlling and reacting to the transmitted programs, loosely described as *interactive television*. There are different levels of interactivity, and we will take a look at each of them from the most restricted to the most complete.

Teletext.   Teletext is a limited but popular form of interactivity. Choices have to be made numerically by standard remote control. Stock indices, traffic updates, airport arrivals, and weather news are just part of the information base for users to track down that stock, route, airplane, or region important to them. When fantasizing about the possibilities of interactive TV, it can do no harm to realize what has already been successful.

In addition to providing information, teletext is used for selling products. It is very straightforward to convert the interest stimulated by a commercial TV program into sales by simultaneously making specific offers via teletext. If there's a program about painting, the viewer can order a painting set via teletext; if there is a program about a certain country, then travel arrangements can be booked. A limitation is the waiting time created by the carousel delivery.

Direct Response TV.   A totally different, but equally simple and accepted form of interaction is using a commercial to get people to call a specific telephone number. It is actually like coupon advertising via the TV. This principle can appear in different forms.

The so-called DRTV commercial is better known in the United States than in Europe, but is also making progress there. The best response is achieved with daytime television, with short commercial blocks, and preferably with the DRTV advert at the end of that block. DRTV commercials are less appropriate during prime time, since the cost per caller can be prohibitive. The average number of telephone calls per DRTV commercial in the Netherlands is 350 per million viewers, of which 80 percent call within the first 10 minutes. The figures in the United Kingdom for Channel 4 are remarkably similar.

There are also infomercials, which can last up to half an hour. From a technical point of view, they are virtually the same as direct response TV. The same is true for channels that transmit only sales programs such as Home Shopping Network and QVC. We will return to this topic later.

TV Videotex.   TV videotex is an electronic information service. To access it, you simply choose the teletext page shown on the menu. Then you dial a telephone number to gain access to a certain page number that opens up a variety of services. Generally speaking videotex is successful as long as you can find your way through the numerical choices. Some systems use letters corresponding to particular numbers, but this only makes the service more complicated. The costs of and returns from the system make it very difficult to turn videotex into a profitable enterprise.

Near Video-on-Demand.   Increased transmission capacity has made it possible to present different films at a number of times during an evening. Companies operating this system provide the needed decoder. Digital TVs with built-in decoders are becoming available. You can't order a film, as you can with video-on-demand (see below), but you can pick up the film as it "goes by." If enough films are coming by, and each film comes by often enough, the difference with video-on-demand becomes comparatively small. The investment costs for this type of system are considerably lower than for full video-on-demand, so it certainly promises to be a commercially viable option. Subscribers pay for what they watch, described as pay-per-view. With "prebooked pay-per-view," an order has to be placed via a voice-response telephone. With "impulse pay-per-view" the order can be placed simply by the remote control.

Interactive TV.   Various tests have been started, then abandoned, then restarted, all based on the following principle: Picture lines are broadcast in tandem with the television signal. The lines are visible only with a machine, for which the viewer pays. The same gadget is used to send signals back to the computer of the TV producer or station. In this way, the viewer can take part in the transmission by giving answers or stating choices. Companies testing this system believe that it offers a commercially attractive form of interactive TV.

During tests run in Spain, more than 70 percent of the participating households made use of the interactive possibilities to react during transmissions. But financial viability remains an obstacle. So far as we know, the system has not been permanently introduced in Spain.

DirecTV®, a trademark of Hughes Electronic, has introduced interactive television in a digital environment in the United States, South America, and Japan. With the emergence of digital TVs, a whole range of interactivity will become available.

Video-on-Demand.   With video-on-demand the viewer has the equivalent of a video shop at home. At any given moment, the consumer can make a selection and order a film for imme-

diate viewing. A substantial investment in the technical infrastructure is needed to make this possible, and there is growing
doubt among some specialists regarding the economic viability
of the demand concept.

During Time Warner's tests in Orlando, the film was compressed into chunks. For a film lasting one and a half hours,
subscribers are given access for two and a half hours. They
then have the same facilities at their disposal as they would
with a video recorder; they can wind back and forth, or rewind
the tape and play it again. Tests showed that the films had to
be updated twice per week in order to maintain interest: once
before the weekend and once after the weekend. Various
American specialists I talked with believe that it will always be
cheaper to distribute videos with a delivery van than send the
contents over the cable. So far they are right.

Full Interactive Network.   A full interactive network includes
a whole assortment of interactive services that the consumer
can access via the cable; video-on-demand is one of them.
Other services being tested and offered in various ways include:

- Requests for latest news at any time
- Access to libraries
- Interactive distance learning
- Sports and music on demand
- Self-medication at a distance
- Home shopping
- Interactive games that users can play with each other

British Telecom has enlisted a large number of local services,
including museums and advice organizations, for its interactive TV activities in Ipswich.

You may be wondering what a fully interactive network
could finally add to the possibilities on the World Wide Web.
How about an interactive electronic supermarket with a 3-D
interior and products that can be viewed from all angles?
Then there's "Skatekid,"™ a computer-animated figure that

guides customers through a selection of videotapes. Both were designed as test concepts for Time Warner's Full Service Network. Unfortunately, the largest test of all time on the electronic highway ended in 1997. The estimated costs were $100 million, and that was rather excessive for the 4000 Time Warner subscribers who used the system at the height of its popularity. In the 1980s JC Penney ran another large-scale test on the electronic highway for home shopping. It too was stopped, for exactly the same reason: The costs per transaction were a multiple of what they should have been. And there was little indication of any improvement. I fear that Time Warner's Full Service Network is not the last failure in electronic home services. Enthusiasm is costly.

Other forms of interactive TV show more promise. Systems such as Open TV (a trademark of Thomson Sun Interactive) and Media Highway (Canal Plus) do not supply video-on-demand, but they can be used for home banking and access to the library. The remote control and a modem included in the digital set-top box or decoder identifies the viewer, who can then make a number of basic transactions. These systems are now being exploited commercially, just like DirecTV®.

Web TV, CD-i.   One related development of historical value is Philips' CD-i. The CD-i player was designed as an addition to home audio and video equipment, and was thus typically consumer-oriented. Yet it was not an interactive application of the television itself. Rather, it was an independent piece of equipment—effectively, a PC disguised for the general consumer. It can be compared to a video recorder, or better, to a variant of the CD player for audio CDs.

The CD-i disk and its player, connected to the TV, formed the first medium able to provide "full-screen motion video" on a disk. Additionally, the CD-i Internet Kit brought the Internet to the television screen. The kit supports three Internet functions: e-mail, newsgroups, and the World Wide Web. New CD-i titles will be equipped with on-line facilities. To be able to use the Internet via CD-i, you need to have a subscription. If this product comes to Europe, it will be called CD-Online;

in the United States, it is called Web-I. High-quality still pictures and films can be read from the disk in the player, and additional topical information can be transferred via the telephone. This in fact constitutes a sort of Videotex with no limitation for visual possibilities. You need not be computer-literate to be able to work fully interactively with excellent picture and sound quality. The success is still to be proved.

However, you still need a disk to start with. That is not necessarily a problem; the need for a tangible and addressable object that can be used as a corporate gift to be sent or sold provides in itself a whole range of possibilities.

Despite all these possibilities—or perhaps because of them—CD-i has never become a commercial success. In professional markets, Coca-Cola, l'Oréal, MacDonald's, car manufacturers, banks, and publishers use CD-i for training personnel and for internal and external communication. However, technical advances come so thick and fast that the PC has already overtaken the possibilities offered by the CD-i. As we have seen, technical superiority during the start-up phase of a product does not necessarily indicate commercial superiority. Philips had a similar earlier experience with its video standard. In order to be successful with such products, it is essential to create a world standard, even if you have to give away the product for nothing. This has more to do with marketing than with production.

Philips' advertising slogans over the years demonstrate the extent to which its main concern is with product rather than with market: "From sand to client" (pointing out the origin of the microchip), "Philips invents for you," and "Let's make things better" all belie a manufacturer's concern. The last one may be excellent for an internal motivational campaign, but again it projects a production-oriented rather than market-oriented approach. Such slogans do not build a household name. One thing you have to admit: Philips is consistent.

Will It Happen at All?   There seem to be just as many people who believe that developments in the TV and PC worlds will turn out to be nothing more than a blip as there are people who are convinced of their certain success. Naturally, devotees are generally more confident about developments in their own sector. Not too many computer freaks are enthusiastic about interactive TV. Similarly, people from the world of consumer electronics maintain that the PC will never make it with the folks who can hardly use a video recorder—and that's the majority. At the moment, no one is right. As all these developments converge, it is not at all certain what the successful forms will be.

America's powerful cable company, Telecommunications Inc. (TCI), made strategic investments in telephone companies in order to exploit the potential of telephony and data communication and to offer Internet access via cable television. However, the company has never been successful in integrating the cable and telephone companies. In 1997, TCI decided to go "back to basics." Former director John Malone admitted that he made a mistake by gambling on the combination of cable TV, speech-and-data communication, and the Internet.

The future of the Internet on TV screens has been a topic of conflicting market research. Dataquest concluded that Internet TV remains too difficult for the consumer, while Yankelovich Partners found that consumers would prefer to surf the Web via TV than via PC. Again, we must view with caution what consumers say about their intended behavior with new media. It is best to follow developments in the age-old medium of the newspaper, with this chapter serving as background. Look at the facts: The growing penetration of CD-ROMs and the Internet, and the increasingly powerful PCs seem to end up in people's living rooms, while at the office you have to make do with old-fashioned setups. Remember, too, it can happen very fast: *In the United States the penetration of television in 1950 was 10 percent; five years later it was 67 percent.* The following section may help point the way.

TELEPHONE, CABLE, AND SATELLITE

The very nature of the transportation facilities—telephone, cable, and/or satellite—is one of the most important factors defining the extent to which a new medium approaches the ideal form. The standard two-way telephone line is quite "narrow," but (moving) pictures can be sent with additional technical facilities. ADSL (Asymmetric Digital Subscriber Line) is one such facility, allowing telecommunications companies to compete with cable companies in terms of bits per second or bandwidth. ADSL provides a connection speed of up to 6MB/second to the client, and a 640KB/second connection from the client back to the provider. Both ends of the old-fashioned copper cables need to be adapted, creating an obstacle for mass penetration. Other facilities just need an ISDN connection (ISDN-DSL) but are much slower (128KB/second). Broadband ISDN, based on asynchronous transfer mode (ATM), is compatible with the actual ISDN and enables full multimedia use.

If media are connected to the cable network, then many bits and bytes can go in one direction. But sending information in the opposite direction requires a special two-way addressable cable. Even then the result is not a comprehensive, balanced network. The combination of cable (for transmission to the customer) and telephone (for sending information from user to supplier) is another option. In the current situation, full two-way communication for voice and data transmission via satellite is not a problem. Videoconferencing is a two-way application for sending video images.

Even options have options. Small wonder that broadcast and cable transmission systems are doing an about-face every decade. TV signals once picked up from the airwaves with antennas now come to us through a cable. Then again, the transponders on satellites—the reflecting mirrors—project footprints at certain regions, where people can pick up the signal with their own satellite dishes. This direct-to-home or direct broadcast satellite (DBS) reception is transmitted through the air. On the other hand, telephone traffic, which traditionally passes through cables in the ground, is taking to the airwaves as mobile communication penetrates the mass consumer markets. But where cable companies are planning to offer telephone services, as is now the case in parts of the United Kingdom, most of the traffic can once again be channeled through the ground—certainly when the cables are connected into worldwide networks. As all these developments converge, one point is certain: The price of sending a certain number of bits per second will fall.

Figure 3-3 compares selected "old" and "new" media, and the ways they are transmitted, with the ultimate form of new media: the sending of data, sound, and video pictures and the

Old Media			
	TELEPHONE	TV	BASIC PC WITH MODEM
From/to everyone	V	—	V
Data	V	V	V
Sound	V	V	—
Video	—	V	—
Transactions	V	—	V

New Media		
	MULTIMEDIA PC WITH MODEM AND CONNECTED TO A NETWORK	TV WITH DECODER AND REMOTE CONTROL
From/to everyone	V	limited/V
Data	V	V
Sound	V	V
Video	→V	V
Transactions	V (safety)	limited/V

Three Ways of Transport			
	NETWORK	SATELLITE	CABLE
From/to everyone	V	—	→V
Data	V	V	V
Sound	V	V	V
Video	→V	V	V
Transactions	V	V	→V

FIGURE 3-3. Mode of communication and capability of old and new media. V = possible; — = not possible; →V = almost possible.

possibility of finalizing transactions. All traditional media fail to fulfill at least one multimedia function; the telephone comes closest to being the ultimate. Among new media it is obvious that the PC and the TV, with their respective peripherals, are very similar. The comparison of the three means of transport shows why network services such as CompuServe® and America OnLine® are competitors to the broadcast companies. The functions and potential of the two media are becoming increasingly similar.

WHAT A MEDIUM MUST BE CAPABLE OF DOING: THE IMPACT

In the previous section we examined the technical components of the media revolution. In this section we turn to the characteristics a medium must possess to bring about a transaction. To be effective, a medium must have an impact on confronting us and an opportunity to confront us. In terms of the marketing process, which characteristics make a medium more effective in bringing about trade? What convinces people, and which characteristics of which media can persuade? How well can media influence our minds, our emotions? Even a limited insight here is sufficient to dispel a number of preconceptions.

Chapter 1 describes the three principal forms by which economic exchange can be realized: premises, people, and media. This chapter examines the widely varying characteristics of different media in relation to these three forms. A printed bank statement sent to our home has a very different effect from a computer information touch screen that presents us with a range of possibilities through attractive images and sounds. They are both media, but the form of presentation, the possibilities, and the way in which we are confronted with them are as different as chalk from cheese.

To determine the potential impact of a medium, we will look at three different dimensions:

• How personal a medium is

- To what extent the medium is interactive
- Which senses are stimulated and to what extent

HOW PERSONAL?

The impact of a medium can vary considerably, depending on the extent to which it is tailored to its audience. How personal it is depends just as much on the way it addresses its target as on the content of the message. "To the inhabitants of this house" is surely less appealing than "To Mr. P. G. Postma"—unless the information happens to be about my house. The attention that the eye gives to personal variables is the reason that name, address, and other individual details are included in some direct mailings. A car number plate or a date of birth will trigger immediate recognition. The person's name does not always have to be used to make the medium seem personal. "Dear nature lover" and "To our friends in Canada" can have considerable impact by relating the reader personally to the sender.

The content of the message can also vary—and should—from impersonal to personal. The regional weather forecast, for example, doesn't depend on who is requesting it. A special offer could apply equally to everyone or be specifically directed at a certain person. Sometimes information is solely of interest if it is individually tailored. Think again about your bank balance. *If you want to know whether a certain check has cleared, you will have little interest in learning that 80 percent of checks are processed in the middle of the month.*

The impact of personalization depends on the nature of the information. A consumer who has given some thought to buying a new car will read a personal invitation for a test drive with much more interest than someone who is not even considering such a purchase. On the other hand, a "supercheap offer" does not necessarily have to be "Just for you, Mr. Postma." It can just as well apply to everybody and be delivered as bulk printed material. Thus function as well as costs must be taken into account in considering the extent to which a medium has to be personally tailored. The more possibilities that a medium provides for individually tailored information, the stronger its commercial influence can be.

HOW INTERACTIVE?

The term *interactivity* is used almost indiscriminately to describe developments in multimedia PCs and in TV. Interaction implies mutual responsiveness, and it is an essential part of human communication: Somebody says something, someone else reacts, the first adapts to the reaction, and so on. When computer interaction changes from limited text-based forms to sense-based visual transmission or even transfer of moving pictures, the word *interactive* will have made its debut in the world of PCs. With TV, this will happen when viewers can participate in games or react to programs other than by writing or making a phone call. Nevertheless, writing and phoning are forms of interaction.

To fulfill its function in bringing about trade, a medium must always provide some way to react, which in turn leads to action from the other end, and so on. In this sense, an advertisement with a reply coupon is interactive: The interested party can react by sending in the coupon. But the interactivity flies along at postal delivery speed, and the usual name for it is "responding." A balance, price, or availability may easily have changed in the interim.

The time for communication back to the supplier can be reduced to practically zero by telephone, especially if voice-response computers are used. Via the voice system, the supplier can let the customer know on-line the account balance and latest transactions, whether products are available, and the current prices. It is the ideal scenario for high probability of use: a relatively cheap method of on-line, two-way communication via a familiar medium that enjoys virtually 100 percent penetration. No wonder that call centers, with combinations of voice-response systems, computer telephone integration, and/or e-mail, enjoy enormous popularity. Catalogs that offer a clear choice from thousands of possibilities or other printed supplements make the system especially attractive. When downtime for transmission of the message is minimal, interactivity takes on a whole new dimension.

We can now distinguish the following components of interactivity:

- The speed of the reaction (by mail vs. immediate)
- Whether the information is up to date ("the information was correct when it was printed," vs. "the information is correct as you see, hear, or read it now")
- The content of the reaction (yes or no vs. detailed order with payment)

There are, of course, gradations within the given extremes. By its nature, a printed medium has a low level of interactivity. The speed is low, and the information—goods offered, prices, bank balances—is not necessarily fully up to date. A mail-order company's catalog is usually valid for six months, and bank statements are typically sent every month. Whether the goods are available when the customer opens the catalog or whether the balance is still correct when the client looks at the statement remains to be seen. By contrast, an on-line connection with a system that provides up-to-date information offers a high level of interactivity. In some applications, such as an electronic request for a bank balance, the client has no need for any reaction. A client who wishes to transfer funds immediately may do so via the same medium. Action, reaction, and instructions that lead to change are all possible.

Sometimes a considerable level of interactivity is implied without an on-line connection. For example, some CDs offer every conceivable choice, so that the end of a film can be altered without having to connect up with anything, since all the variations are contained on the disk. In all cases, when up-to-date information has to be requested or an order sent, a connection is essential and the level of interactivity is heightened.

In short, interactivity depends on the speed and flexibility of information exchange, whether the information is up to date, and the content of the reaction. The level of interactivity is highest when secure payments must be made. These are important criteria for determining the significance of a medium in the marketing process and for estimating the potential impact of a medium in the commercial process.

WHICH SENSES ARE STIMULATED?

The extent to which the barrage of stimuli that reach our senses can be turned into digital information, has a direct bearing on the influence of a medium and thus its commercial function. A customer can see, hear, feel, smell, and taste the products in a shop, and the sales assistant can by word and action exert a lot of influence on the customer. The stimuli created by the newest electronic media mimic this environment. Alongside the superb digital reproduction of sound, we now have full-screen, moving-picture video, a very powerful audiovisual instrument for attracting a customer. *There is nothing the human nervous system desires more than color video pictures with sound.* In principle, the sense of touch can be stimulated with a data glove. Experiments have been carried out with the sense of smell by mail order companies. For example, pages in a catalog advertising leather goods can be made to smell of leather. To what extent this technique will be developed further remains to be seen. The sense of taste has yet to be stimulated via media.

Emotions are stimulated best with audiovisual images: high-quality full-screen video. The power of interactive TV could well lie here. So, too, does the challenge to create interactivity. Interactivity via PC and modem is high, but is limited by the power of the individual user's PC and the speed of the modem. Time is bound to see progress.

AN IDEAL MIX OF THREE DIMENSIONS

The Marketing Media Cube®, shown in Figure 3-4, highlights the three dimensions that determine a medium's potential within the marketing function: degree of personalization, degree of interactivity, and sensory stimulation. Depending on the function that a medium has to fulfill in the commercial process, the relevant characteristics can be looked up in the Marketing Media Cube®. We are concerned with combinations of these three dimensions.

The extent to which technology plays a role becomes obvious if we fill in the three dimensions, as shown in Figure 3-5. Information technology is clearly essential once there is any level of individually tailored communication. In principle, the reply coupon can fulfill its function without a computer. But as soon as any component that entails interactivity is required, automation becomes essential. The stimulation of the senses is also limited without information technology. All things considered, only the media situated in the front left quadrant of the cube can manage without an IT component.

To illustrate, the Marketing Media Cube® in Figure 3-4 is divided into eight numbered blocks, with the three dimensions varying from "low" to "high" levels. Media and media combinations can be filled in for each of the blocks. For audiovisual media, however, pillars consisting of two blocks are needed:

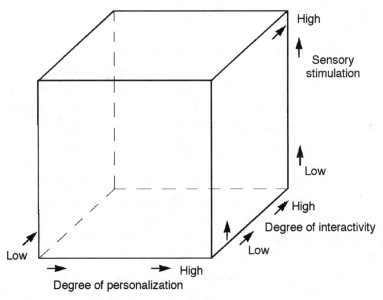

FIGURE 3-4. The Marketing Media Cube®.

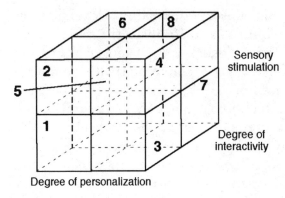

FIGURE 3-5.   Eight blocks in the Marketing
Media Cube®.

audio media in the upper blocks and visual media in those
below.

As an example, the front left section of the cube (block 1)
could include ads with reply coupons, house-to-house mailings and folders, nonselectively distributed pamphlets, and
catalogs. They are not personalized, not very interactive, and
restricted to the visual communication of text and static
images. Applied correctly, however, these relatively simple
media can be extraordinarily effective.

At the other extreme, examine the back right of the cube
(blocks 7 and 8) with the combinations of image and sound
carriers, controlled by a multimedia PC and connected to a
central system with up-to-date information from the supplier.
Connecting a card reader allows the user to be identified and
payments to be made; in the United States, entering a credit
card number is sufficient if no card reader is available.
Applications and experiments with "home access shopping"—
the combined efforts of cable, telephone, and entertainment
companies—can be placed in this area of the cube. A CD
with a modem connection is an example. Between these two
extremes, every possible form of media and combination of
media can be filled in according to their potential within the
commercial process.

Figure 3-6 shows various media that can be used for direct marketing. The numbers in parentheses refer to the blocks in Figure 3-5; in this way, the various media can be positioned in the cube. The division between media that reach us in print and media that reach us via loudspeakers and/or screens— here shown as electronic—has farther-reaching marketing consequences than is immediately apparent. In terms of what a medium can achieve in the commercial process, each has opposite but important strengths.

1. Print media may seem unsensational in the new marketing era, but they have one important characteristic that electronic media lack: *Print media induce action, even if that action is just to throw the paper away.* No matter what, a mailing delivered to your door has to be picked up. You are forced to confront the envelope, if nothing else. Most likely,

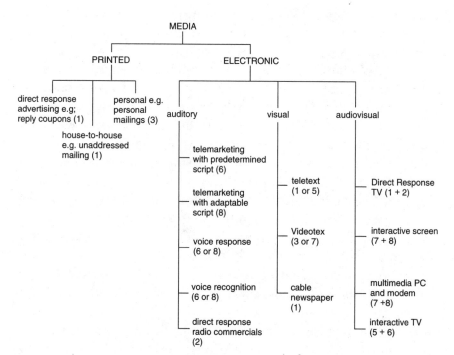

FIGURE 3-6. Media for direct marketing.

you will open it, just to take a glance at the contents. For once there might be something important inside. Research by the Dutch post office shows that mailings have considerable recall value. People may complain that they "throw the junk away," but the trick is that they want to know what they are tossing. With electronic media, people must be switched on, in the first place. The supplier of a product can force target users to pick up an envelope from the doormat, but cannot force them to turn on an electronic medium, let alone make sure they choose the right channel or site. In that sense, electronic media are passive, except for e-mail in an electronic in-box and outgoing telephone calls.

2. One of the determining elements for interactivity is whether the information is up to date. By definition, print media are only as accurate as the date they come off the presses. On the contrary, with electronic media, the information can be read on-line and therefore is correct at any given time.

Telemarketing in which people follow standard scripts occupies a somewhat special place in this arena. In effect, personal intervention is carried out in such a way that the whole process has all the characteristics of a (costly) direct-marketing solution. Outbound telemarketing can combine the strong points of printed and electronic media: It is possible to provide on-line information, tailored to the person being called and with very rapid reactions in both directions. At the same time, the outbound call forces a confrontation. Using a voice-response computer to make the call offers on-line information and forced confrontation without the need for personal intervention. Inventiveness in this area could lead to surprising solutions.

In practice, the key issue is not creating a medium that can do as much as possible, but discovering a medium or combination of media that can do as much as is required for the job—or better still, finding a new or improved application that is better than what is already in use. People do not have to wait for the newest of the new in order to be successful.

A good example is a catalog combined with a voice-response computer. The catalog attractively introduces the full selection of goods into the customer's home. The client's queries about the price, availability, and delivery time for a product can be communicated without personal intervention through the voice-response computer. The strong points of each medium are tapped to full potential, while the weaker points of one (minimal interactivity; minimal stimulation of the senses) are offset by the other. The catalog and the voice-response computer are ideal complementary media. The oft-predicted demise of the catalog will just have to wait a while.

As new media are developed, the functions they bring to the commercial process can be analyzed and updated through the Marketing Media Cube®.

THREE FACTORS EXPLAIN MEDIA SUCCESS

The technical attributes and marketing possibilities of a medium must be carefully attuned. Numerous successes have been predicted—predictions based on technical possibilities—but they have not yet materialized, usually because the commercial potential is judged far too superficially. Even so, the chance of success is determined not only by technical possibilities and their commercial function, but also by three groups of factors:

- The hardware
- The environment
- The user

FAMILIAR HARDWARE

The required hardware simply has to be available to the potential user. Equipment can exist in a test phase, or it can be available for the enthusiast, but that says nothing about its actual accessibility to potential clients. Too often enthusiasm at the test stage is so great that existing or targeted penetration is not calculated realistically.

Deadlock: The Chicken or the Egg.   Lack of market penetration is often labeled a chicken-or-egg situation. That is, the equipment will not take off if its functions are not appreciated, and its functions will not be realized unless the equipment is there. Inevitably there is an attempt to break the deadlock with so-called brainstormings where everyone concerned tries to find an answer. Such an initiative was undertaken at the time to introduce Minitel, the French Internet predecessor, in various countries outside of France. However, these approaches have not been successful because this was not a chicken-or-egg situation: There was simply no market opportunity because Minitel is as French as a baguette. No market existed outside France. Within centrally governed France itself it was possible to force a breakthrough because of the obvious business interests.

Generally, this kind of situation is not a chicken-or-egg question, but simply a *lack of opportunity.* Therefore there is no deadlock, merely interesting ideas that are apparently not viable. If a product is forced to emerge against market wishes, it most probably will not emerge at all. Market penetration must be monitored carefully. Organic growth is the best yardstick. Consider the natural market development of goods and services that seem to survive without enormous subsidies and government intervention. A typical example of unstructured, unpredictable, and nonsubsidized but massive growth is the Internet. Another example is the mushrooming growth in television channels. Even in Europe, with its traditionally limited number of government-subsidized channels, there has been an explosion in the deregulated, commercial arena.

Price, Portability, and Availability.   The degree of penetration for equipment is directly related to the price. The lower the price, the easier the penetration, as modems and PCs illustrate. The freedom provided by portable equipment (mobility) greatly stimulates market penetration, as we have seen with the mobile telephone. Availability also plays a key role. Is the equipment available, without restriction, to the intended user? Restrictions in business markets may differ somewhat from those in consumer markets. In principle, a computer terminal with tourist information is available 24 hours per day, 7 days per week, but it will primarily be used during the tourist season when the weather is promising. Even then, only one person can use it at a time. Another form of restricted availability arises when the mass media invite people to make an electronic response. Then the peak load on the telephone lines is the bottleneck.

LOGICAL SURROUNDINGS

Place of use can be an extremely important factor in assessing a product's chances of success. Information points and kiosks are available if the client leaves the house, but often the equipment is most useful or only useful if it is available at home. "Public access" has to be weighed against "home access." With public access, the actual surroundings play a critical role. Do users understand what the equipment is meant for? Do they physically come across it when they are prepared to make a purchase? Are privacy and safety guaranteed?

A good example of a public access purchasing medium is the automatic ticket machine found in many railway stations. The surroundings are perfectly suited to the function: The station is ideal for the sale of train tickets. In principle, tickets could also be sold at a post office, but it is questionable whether people would buy them there, or even think about it. In addition, availability is ensured if there are enough ticket machines, so that the last group of factors—those pertaining to the user (see below)—are satisfactorily fulfilled. Finally, the chances of success are strengthened by the fact that these are generally the only circumstances under which train tickets can be purchased, although it would be dangerous to put all your money on that fact. After all, people can still take the car!

NO SECRET FOR JOE BOGGS

The chances of success are very small when factors affecting the typical user are underestimated or incorrectly assessed. Good reason therefore to give Joe Boggs some thought.

New transactions.   To start with, do not underestimate the barrier that has to be broken down if you are to teach people new things. This might mean pushing an unfamiliar button— the star (*) or pound (#) key on a telephone, for example. Services that use these buttons can be difficult to market. With one of the first large-scale voice-response systems in Europe, the ordering service of Wehkamp mail-order company in the Netherlands, the pound key had to be used to complete every series of numbers; it worked as the "enter" signal. Even though the dialogue was scripted to remind people to do so— and the catalog showed larger-than-life images of the symbol on virtually every page—four out of five clients forgot to use the key. The system made a breakthrough only when the symbol no longer had to be used. *Introducing a new action on existing equipment poses an enormous hurdle.* In business and industrial markets, this hurdle is usually easier to overcome, but it is still true that the actions required should be those with which the user is familiar.

That the hurdle can grow into a towering wall if the equipment in question is unfamiliar needs no elaboration. Once again, solutions tend to be easier in business markets. A dealer who can order parts only with a certain application simply learns how to use the relevant equipment. But forced learning is by no means an excuse to produce something that is difficult to use.

Structure and content of dialog.   Direct marketers who are accustomed to increasing their turnover via a printed medium know how critical the text is in a coupon advertisement, mailing, or catalog. The creation of texts and layout to produce a favorable response for a reasonable cost per order is a specialization in itself, about which there are plenty of publications.[5] The structure of an electronic dialogue, by its very transitory nature, has to satisfy at least the same criteria as those for printed media. We will return to this topic in Chapter 4.

With printed media, people can turn back to a page relatively easily, look for the folded corners, or scribble in the margins. With electronic media, this is all a lot trickier; the structure and the content of the dialogue has to be so carefully designed that people simply cannot make mistakes. And rarely is this the case. The automatic ticket machines in railway stations—at least those in France, including the English-language version—are an exception. It is very easy to see the role of Minitel as a forerunner of this mass medium.

No Instructions Required.   The user has to experience the equipment, format, and dialogue in such a way that no instruction manual is required. When people do the most obvious thing, the equipment should react in the desired fashion. On the automatic ticket machine mentioned earlier, the instructions state quite simply: touch the screen. Anyone who does this can't go wrong; the dialogue leads the way.

To reach your prospects more effectively, keep in mind that very often *beautiful and original concepts only seem completely useless.* The human eye follows a certain sequence in its examination of objects and text, as has been established by skimming of newspapers and reading of mailings. Ergonomists can also make a valuable contribution. Many successful new media applications are developed by computer specialists in cooperation with graphic designers. It is amazing how often even large companies, in their enthusiasm, repeatedly overlook the professionalism that has been amassed by direct-marketing practitioners in this field.

Only when problems with the equipment, the surroundings, and the user are solved in an attractive way will the chances for success be heightened. Contrary to the claims of many champions of new media, the much-lauded "ease of access" is totally inadequate to ensure success. People go into a shop, not because it is safe or easy to enter, but because the attraction proves irresistible. The same applies to an electronic medium. The service offered has to be irresistibly attractive in order to be successful, and that is quite different from not being difficult to use.

MEDIA AND THE NEW MARKETING ERA

Thus far, we have looked at the enormous increase in technical possibilities, the consequent impact that media can have on the marketing process, and the factors that determine success with respect to equipment, environment, and user. Let us now turn to the long- and short-term significance of new media for marketing and business management.

MATCHING THE TRENDS

A number of trends in our society can be important for commercial behavior. Let us look at a few.

From the Masses to the Individual.   Much has been written about the trend toward increasing individualization in society. In economic terms, the "faceless" society came about during the industrial revolution, when mass-produced goods could be sold without much difficulty because of universal shortages. The population explosion after World War II culminated in unprecedented mass production and consumption. The "old school" of marketing, more or less derived from economic sciences, established such well-known concepts as the price elasticity of demand, the pricing mechanism, and consumer models—all based on rational behavior. As a result, target groups were defined within this mass market, each with its respective consumption patterns and associated brands.

Before the industrial revolution, peddlers carried larger pots and pans to those areas where there were lots of children and smaller pots and pans to areas where there were few children. Now, thanks to information technology, sellers can once again knock on the door with a tailormade product. The demassification of society renews the desire for one-to-one business transactions, all made possible by the revolutions in information and media. This does not mean that there are no longer any viable product/market combinations for mass marketing. It does mean that there is a choice between the mass approach and the large-scale, individualized approach for mass markets.

Philosophers talk about the growth of an ego culture in the western world, where enjoyment of life, self-fulfillment, and satisfaction through personal success are highly valued. Self-realization is more important than being part of the whole. Consumption pressure directed at the masses does not necessarily fit in with these ideas. Instead of the old order, with everybody wanting the same thing, there is a new pattern with everybody seeking something different. Those who are accustomed to using the mass approach will see the new markets as chaotic. But there is in fact another order—the individual order—overlaying though not obliterating the old mass patterns. Manufacturers of mass-produced consumer goods can continue to view much of the market as a mass market. In my opinion, it will be important to treat only major customers on an individual level to be certain of the relationship. Companies will be able to rely much less on brand loyalty alone.

The trend toward individualization can also be seen at the macro level: Governments decentralize activities by contracting them out to smaller, privatized departments; this applies to a whole selection of activities, ranging from basic utilities to trash collection. Companies are shifting responsibility farther down the hierarchical ladder: from centralized organizations to business units with their own objectives and greater emphasis on individual responsibilities.

From Generic to Specific. The trend toward individualization is linked to the trend toward hunting down goods and services tailored to the consumer. One holiday home fits the bill; the other definitely does not. One current account is handier than the other. The product assortment can swell enormously with no additional revenue to compensate. But information technology can also offer a helping hand here. A modular product range can ensure that the customer has a large choice, while the supplier has to produce only a limited number of variants.

From Limited Choice to Abundance. Individualization and specification lead to an abundance of choices. Whether you're buying furniture, a CD, or a car, you encounter a confusing range of diversity. If you open a car magazine from the 1960s, you will find the whole range of prices offered on a single page. In today's car magazines, the price list extends for three packed pages—and often that covers only the basic models. The diversity plays into the hands of the new media; they can perform a search function that was not needed when the world was still orderly.

From Print to Electronic.   Media alarmists who foresee the demise of books in the home, in favor of electronic information carriers, understand little about recent developments. We have probably never had so many books at home as we will have in five years' time. But we will also have more electronic information in the house, and the growth of the latter will exceed that of the former. So much for predictions of a paperless office as well. The workplace has never been so inundated with paper.

A similar paradox has emerged with cash and electronic money. Despite the greater use of electronic payments, the amount of cash in circulation—coins and notes—is increasing. And how. Paper simply has a new sidekick: electronic forms of information, money, amusement, and relaxation that we previously did not have.

From Passive to Interactive.   The addition of electronic media to print media leads from a passive acquaintance to a direct interaction between sender and receiver. Electronic users can react directly to the exchange rates, the weather, or the price. As the level of action and interaction increases, users come to feel that they can exercise more influence as individuals. They no longer have to wait for things to come along or be decided. They can act, direct, and choose for themselves.

From Plenty of Time to Fast, Faster, Fastest.   In western society, time is money. Short delivery times and quick reactions are high on the list of priorities. The feeling is more prevalent in the United States than in Europe, and more in urban areas than in the countryside. All in all, the customer is not a terribly patient creature. Some writers propose that time is becoming the most significant factor in competition.[6] New consumer product variations, including the house brands of chain stores, are copied by the competition within a few months or even weeks.

Not 9 to 5, but 24-Hour. The "time is money" experience leads to a decreasing tolerance for closing times. Clients want to be able to do business at any time of the day, and any day of the week. Banks and other financial services, which until a few years ago had very restricted opening times in both the United States and Europe, actually seem to be taking the lead. Retail, travel, and other service industries are tending toward longer opening times. As usual, the 24-hour economy has penetrated the United States much more quickly than Europe, but there too it is fast taking hold.

If we compare these trends with the possibilities offered by the new media, there seems to be an almost perfect match. It is almost as if the new media were created to respond to everything that individualization involves: personally addressed offers and efficient searches through disorderly quantities and varieties of information. In fact, the new media are both the products of individualizing, interactive, electronic trends and the vehicles that make the realization of these trends possible.

The speed of business can be increased significantly through the appropriate use of electronic media. The fax is a remarkable device. It has been around for several decades, but it has achieved considerable market penetration only in the last few years. With this fairly old-fashioned but particularly easy-to-use piece of equipment, a letter is received the moment it is sent. Using the PC to send messages fulfills the same function and eliminates the need for printing. But the required actions—in particular, loading the software and using it for the first time—are just a little less self-evident. This slightly more intimidating barrier is obviously enough to make people prefer the fax. As the number of PCs sold with a modem and required software increases, and as the Internet grows in popularity, e-mail will become more widespread. Again, don't assume that the fax or PC means the end of postal traffic. On the contrary. Postal traffic increases, because when a document is sent by fax the original is generally sent on by mail. People are not so easily weaned from their old habits. As with cash, books, and paper in the office, electronics will not supersede everything, but will offer additional possibilities.

"Business hours" are more easily extended via media sales than via sales representatives or shops and showrooms. Costs are reduced as well. It is far less expensive to funnel concentrated demand to a single (phone) number, where all the relevant information is available, than to open a chain of shops for longer hours.

In short, the new media are a gift from the gods of commerce. They fit in very well with a large number of social trends that are important for business. In fact, the new media are self-sustaining, generating ever-increasing demands from clients that only the media themselves can satisfy.

SHORT-TERM FUNCTIONS

Where should you start today with new media in the day-to-day running of your business or organization? To gain some idea of what is required, you can simply make an inventory of all your business activities and carefully list the specific characteristics you consider essential to the success of your organization. Then you can tick off whether, how, and to what extent the new media can perform these functions and strengthen specific characteristics.

To assist in this process, Figure 3-7 lists a number of commercial functions for various products and services. An X indicates whether a function for those particular products or services can be performed especially well through media. A dash (—) suggests this is not the case, and a question mark (?) means a media solution is not particularly obvious or could go either way.

Two functions are ideal candidates for media solutions, no matter what the product: searching for interested prospects, otherwise known as lead generation, and maintaining a relationship with the client. In mass markets, these activities should be limited to important customers—the heavy users—

	CHAT SERVICES AND GAMES	FINANCIAL SERVICES	CARS	CLOTHING	MASS CONSUMER GOODS
Lead generation	x	x	x	x	x
Inventory	x	x	?	?	—
Distribution	x	x	—	—	—
Payment	x	x	?	?	—
Showing the product	x	?	?	?	?
Exchange	x	x	—	—	—
Customer loyalty	x	x	x	x	x

FIGURE 3-7.   New media and their suitability according to product and function in the business process.

because of costs and revenue. For the remaining functions, appropriateness depends very much on the product in question.

For games and chat services, supply and distribution coincide; participation is the supply and theoretically is limitless. Payment can be collected from the charge for the telephone connection and therefore runs in tandem with supply. The use of all media possibilities encapsulates the supply in a virtual world.

Financial services have no supply problems. *Six-month fixed-deposit savings accounts are never sold out.* Transferring money into an account means that payment has been made and distribution completed, although a written statement generally follows. Changing your account to, say, a 12-month deposit is no problem whatsoever and can be done via the same medium. The presentation of services is not especially exciting for the financial sector; this is also true of print media. Anything is possible.

Electronic media can be used very effectively in the production of made-to-order physical goods such as cars and clothing. Less advantage is to be gained with products in stock. Change can be indicated by removing the images of sold-out products from the medium, but this is little different from taking products off the shelves in the shop. Physical goods have to be physically distributed, so new media offer no advantage here. Electronic payment systems have to be sufficiently secure, or a direct payment system is needed such as that used by mail-order companies.

New media are especially effective in showing ranges. For example, if cars are available in many models, the images, components, and prices could be manipulated until the customer has put together an ideal version. Clothes can also be shown in a large number of ways. Customers could scan in their photos, and punch in their measurements, to see themselves in the various styles offered. In principle, they are getting made-to-measure clothes. But extra effort is required from the supplier; that is why "showing the product" is listed as questionable in Figure 3-7.

Whenever consulting the media is the same as delivery of the goods or service, electronic presentations are ideal. This is true even if a stream of paper-confirming transactions has to follow (as with banks and insurers). The need for physical delivery of goods negates some of the advantages. Moreover, physical distribution will not necessarily become cheaper because of developments in computing and media. At best, route-planning systems can be put to use automatically if customers type in their orders via a medium. Weekly grocery shopping is not particularly suited to media sales or teleshopping. It is nothing more than a special form of service, for which there is a market in its own right. When images and sound are combined via the Internet, sound recordings can be effectively sold by sampling. This is a great possibility for the sale of CDs.

When the characteristics of goods and services make selling via the new media particularly attractive, the question becomes whether the existing large-scale suppliers have a market for their product. If they do, small or start-up companies are highly likely to jump into such a niche. Let us look at a few examples.

Articles that are primarily attractive because of the way they are presented can be sold very well through impressive audiovisual media. The effect is comparable to people demonstrating products in department stores or at trade shows. The presentation can be strengthened by affirming that the product is not available elsewhere. The medium therefore claims exclusivity. Another form of product demonstration arises when there is a strong concentration of specific customers at certain times via a certain medium. This concentration lends itself to offers aimed at that particular group. Children who sit in front of the television on Sunday mornings watching the concentration of toys being advertised are a prime example.

The "buy or die" principle can also work very well via the media. The principle concerns very emphatic offers—such as one-time-only or "last call" sales—mostly in combination with other selling points mentioned above. The article to be sold is continually on screen. It is not a static picture; rather, the object moves, sparkles, and/or is shown from every angle by the camera. The price is very attractive compared with the supposed retail price, and there is a "presenter" who talks on enthusiastically while satisfied customers sing the praises of the article. Finally, the fast-decreasing number of articles still available is displayed at the bottom of the screen. It is a kind of auction via media. Home Shopping Network and QVC are two examples of this kind of selling.

To summarize: In certain circumstances, making purchases via a medium can actually be easier than by other methods. Telebanking is an example in consumer as well as business markets. Other examples include a whole range of mail-order companies for consumer markets (La Redoute, Kays, Otto, and L.L. Bean, for example); books and CD outlets on the Internet (Amazon.com); credit card services; and bookings for vacations. Finally, whenever lead generation and the maintenance of customer relations and customer loyalty are important, media presentations have the advantage. These are precisely the functions that are the battlefield in today's business environment.

THE MARKETING MEDIA MATRIX®

New media create totally new marketing opportunities and fit in perfectly with the trends in today's business environment. But this is not true for all products and for all functions. The issue is not really about replacing or extrapolating from what exists already, but about developing completely new applications. In addition, it is the combination of media and information that gives the new applications their real power.

To demonstrate the power of media in combination with information, Figure 3-8 shows the Marketing Media Matrix®, which can be superimposed on the Marketing Information Matrix® (see Figure 2-1). The vertical axis is the same in both matrices. Here the horizontal axis gives the development from right to left, of the functions served by the media in the commercial process. As with information, the media play an increasingly influential role.

The primary role of media in advertising was and still is to achieve a certain coverage, whether in a mass market or a defined target group. The next step is to create awareness of the advertised product and then determine whether coverage and awareness also lead to a specific preference, a stated intention to buy. For the advertising world, the responsibility ends here. The media go one step further: They realize the purchase.

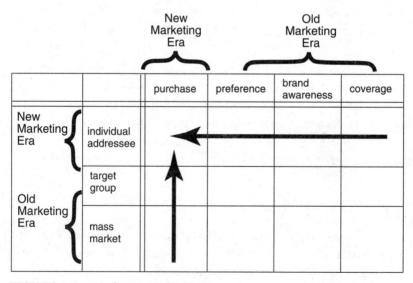

FIGURE 3-8.   Marketing Media Matrix.

Recall from Chapter 1 that the measurable marketing methods include media, people, and premises. New, electronic media are in an increasingly better position to take over the role of the other two methods in bringing about economic exchange. Among traditional media, exchange is possible using coupons, mailings, catalogs, and direct-response commercials—in short, direct marketing. Direct marketing via the new, electronic media comes close to the meaning of *electronic commerce*. From a technical point of view, electronic commerce refers to a group of enabling information technologies that can be used for buying and selling goods and services through the interchange of related data. EDI, which is simply the electronic exchange of data, is also included here. EDI illustrates the combining power of the new electronic possibilities. With the popularization of the Internet and Intranets, EDI has finally found its place.

Through transaction information generated as a result of customers using the media, a whole new marketing reality opens up. Logically deduced and assumed target groups and logically anticipated buying patterns—as defined by traditional marketing techniques—become mere a priori suppositions. How different they turn out to be from the actual target group (if one exists) and its true buying patterns! *The haze of traditional marketing methods has finally been blown away, and what has become visible is a new marketing reality.* The reasons for these surprising discrepancies are revealed in Chapter 4, which also shows how today's commercial processes can be managed more effectively.

NOTES

1. M. McLuhan, *Understanding Media: The Extensions of Man*, MIT Press, Cambridge, Mass., 1964.
2. N. Negroponte, *Being Digital*, Knopf, New York, 1995.
3. Sunil Gupta of the Hermes project at University of Michigan School of Business (sgupta@umich.edu or http://www.umich.edu/—sgupta/hermes.htm) and Kim Pitkow and Mimi Recker of the Graphics, Visualization, and Usability Center's 3d WWW User Survey (http://www.cc.gatech.edu/gvu/user_surveys/).

4. "CD-ROM Consumer Rumble Turns into a Roar," *New Media Strategist,* May 4, 1995; "The Multimedia Wipeout—Why Are CD-Roms Such Bad Business?" *The Economist,* June 15, 1996; "The Great CD-ROM Shakeout," *Marketing Computers,* May 1996.

5. See, for example, S. Vogele, *99 Erfolgsregeln für Directmarketing (99 Rules for Direct Marketing),* Verlag Moderne Industrie, 86895 Landsberg/Lech, Germany, 1995; T. Kok, "Het kijken naar een postordercatalogus" ("Looking at a mail order catalogue"), no. B5250, *Handboek Direct Marketing (Direct Marketing Handbook),* Samsom Business Information, Alphen a/d Rijn, The Netherlands, 1995.

6. G. Gerken, *Abschied vom Marketing (Saying Goodbye to Marketing),* ECON Verlag, Düsseldorf/Vienna/New York, 1992.

FOUR

WE'RE ONLY HUMAN

Thanks to the information and media revolutions, both
information and media will play a much more significant
role in the commercial process. Will this development change
commercial functions and departments within organizations?
Will it change the type of personnel and the form of management? What role will be played by the technocratic approach
and what role will be assumed by feeling or intuition—the
conviction that some irrational choice is the right one? Will
creativity still be allowed?

REVOLUTIONS DON'T AFFECT
SOME THINGS

The problem with revolutionary developments is that the outcome is largely unpredictable. Proponents of the information
revolution think that everything in the world will be put right
once the electronic highway has taken shape: educational
opportunities for everyone, no more traffic jams now that people are working from home, no more trips to town to buy mer-
chandise, and a world of peace and happiness because people
can get whatever they want (albeit only virtually) by sitting in
front of their PCs. Some of these advocates are enthusiastic
users and computer freaks; others are politicians or people
who are in some way professionally involved with informatics.
They share a childlike excitement about future possibilities.
Of course, those who earn their living from speculating on

future scenarios for this sector feel compelled to predict something sensational about a fascinating new world.

At the opposing extreme are people who are well aware of the developments but are unhappy with them. Their views may receive less publicity, but the content of their message is not necessarily less important. These people are concerned about who will control the new know-how, the decline in human skills as computers take over more tasks, unemployment and the growing chasm between the haves and have-nots, and the resulting disintegration of society. The developments in telephony may be fascinating, but if half the world's population has never used a telephone—and a large part of it does not even have enough to eat—a different perspective emerges.

Somewhere in the middle are people who are relatively uninformed of the new developments and therefore feel that it's all a storm in a teacup. Most are convinced that the consequences will not be all that bad.

A hard reality is worth mentioning here. The opinions of experts are not necessarily more valuable than the views of outsiders. When Brian Epstein played the demo tape of a new band to Decca executives in 1962, their expert opinion was that "guitar bands are becoming less and less popular." Columbia Records, Pye, and HMV also saw no future for the group. *After signing a contract with EMI, the band sold 200 million records in six years: The group was the Beatles.* In the same way, Albert Einstein was turned down by the Scientific Institute in Munich "because nothing much would become of him"; Verdi was rejected by the music conservatory in Milan because "he would never end up being above average"; and Rembrandt and his contemporaries were written off by John Ruskin, the leading nineteenth-century English art critic, because "all the colors are wrong." Experts tend to think that the subject in which they specialize will soon take over the world. During the first-ever Delphi investigation, artificial intelligence (AI) experts concluded that widespread application of AI was to be expected in the 1970s. So much for the views of specialists.

In short, experts who sing the praises of future developments, experts who see calamity in the same developments, and people on the street who think everything in the future could turn out to be good or bad all have the same chances of their visions of the future becoming reality. However, watch out for people who think they have a monopoly on wisdom.

Developments in science and technology can be seen as positive or negative, without either interpretation being incorrect. But it is certainly wrong to emphasize one and play down the other. We can travel where we want in comfort. We can talk on the phone with whomever we want wherever they may be. We are sheltered from the elements and can cure dreadful illnesses that once meant certain death. All that is true. At the same time, the environment is being destroyed, we are fighting unsuccessfully against AIDS, 1.5 billion people endure unbearable hunger, and wars are being waged with unprecedented cruelty.

The methods may change, but human desires, whether base or admirable, do not. The lust for power, use of violence, criminal behavior, hatred of foreigners, the desire for revenge, serving self-intrest, to name but a few of the least pleasant examples, will remain with us for all time. People apparently have characteristics and tendencies which have not changed over the centuries. It is not plausible to expect the media and information revolutions to suddenly alter human greed *or* human altruism—even though some of the sketches of the future are based consciously or unconsciously on this belief.

"We no longer go to work, but work comes to us" is one of the best-known observations about the new marketing era. If we look at it critically, we have to acknowledge both sides. In many professions it is technically impossible to carry out work at home—for example, in the nursing and welfare fields. There is also the prosaic restriction of people's domestic circumstances and their family situation, which can limit working at home. But the most important point is that people communicate only partly via digital information that can be sent from home. Much of human communication is analog: gestures and expressions. Later sections of this chapter deal with them in greater detail. The power play in meetings, the corridors where business is discussed, and the informal ways in which business is carried out determine, to a large extent, how successful people are at work. And these things don't happen when we're working at home. The expression "Out of sight, out of mind" sums it up. It is this sort of two-sided coin that the so-called layperson often understands very well.

Are people less superstitious because some simple scientific discoveries have begun to erode commonly held assumptions? Not one bit. As the worldwide spread of information via the Internet improves our technical knowledge, opposite trends also appear. Websites of sects and paranormal aspects of comets may be less popular than websites on sex, but they are still substantial.

Superstitious stories about the comet Hale-Bopp generated a lot of traffic on the Net. "Whether Hale-Bopp has a 'companion' or not is irrelevant from our perspective. However, its arrival is joyously very significant to us at Heaven's Gate," said the New Age Sect Higher Source website before the group's collective suicide in March 1997. Nothing new under the sun since the Middle Ages, one might observe. Simply put, some human tendencies—the need for belief systems and superstitions—cannot be erased by science and technology.

The fact that space exploration has made us a bit more sophisticated about the "heavens" has not changed everyone's way of thinking. And who is to decide whether it should? The faithful and the infirm still flock to the shrine at Lourdes. And although progress in medical science argues against investing in hotels there, that's exactly what shrewd investors should be doing, as it turns out. There are basic human tendencies that cannot be affected by scientific and technological developments.

These unchanging human tendencies are the central issue for those who wish to understand the impact of technology on marketing. That is, human behavior is the essence of marketing: When does someone buy something and why? What are the basic human urges that have apparently withstood evolution to remain part of our very nervous system? If we know something about behavior, we can avoid misinterpreting the consequences of the media and information revolutions.

To have insight into the consequences of both the media and information revolutions for commercial activity, it is, of course, necessary to understand that human behavior has its origins in both evolution (or creation, if you are so inclined) and the effects of environment and education on a human individual's development.

It is a fact that some people quickly resort to violence and others do not. Education, environment, and the conditions under which people are raised are all factors. Experiments have shown the extent to which circumstances can lead to violence in people who don't consider themselves to be violent.[1] A panel of students was divided in two. One group was given one role to play and the other was given a different role. As time went on, one group actually became violent toward the other simply as a result of the role it had been given. The people involved could not explain this, but the violence was certainly observed. Apparently everyone is potentially violent, but the degree to which it is expressed depends to a greater or lesser degree on a variety of factors. Let us compare this relatively innocent experiment with the war in former Yugoslavia; there we can see the same phenomenon on a larger scale. Neighbors, people who had been close friends for years, and even spouses, suddenly developed a deep hatred of one another and dealt with each other in a most appalling manner. And then there's our behavior on the asphalt highway. As drivers, talented managers and respectable parents can suddenly display an aggression that takes on life-threatening proportions. The "us versus them" mentality prevails.

The Greek philosopher Herakleitos observed, "War is the father of all things." More than 2000 years have passed, yet most of the games played on the PC consist of shooting and destroying the enemy! How little has changed! I use this example as an illustration of the type of human tendency which has been evident for centuries, and which can be prompted by external factors. I assume that these tendencies will not change and that when interpreting the revolutions in information and media, we must take into account those urges which are potentially present in everybody. *Those who think that everything will be peaceful on the electronic superhighway and that there will be no aggression, assault, or murder do not understand how people are made.* Human tendencies do not change. What changes is the way we interpret these tendencies. There are even businesspeople who like to say that marketing is war.

The trick in the new marketing era is to recognize the age-old human tendencies that are important in the context of commercial dealings. Because of the turbulent changes in information and media, we must be careful not to make two mistakes:

- The first is to think that new developments will change human tendencies that have persisted through the ages.
- The second is to forget that old forms will coexist alongside new forms.

My 8-year-old daughter often plays computer games at school. But while we were vacationing in a national park, she picked daisies and made them into a chain without any prompting from me or my wife. She simply did exactly as her grandmother must have done before her. Some things never change!

With these behavioral axioms in mind, we can move on to key decision-making processes in the new marketing era. Here two separate issues must be addressed:

1. How were and are decisions made about marketing matters? (supply side)
2. How were and are decisions made about purchasing? (demand side)

The first question looks at business decision making: How well do people make decisions on the basis of information available? How systematically do people think and decide? The second question deals largely with how potential buyers perceive the information in the media and whether they act in the way that the supplier intended. It is about the human being as a buying animal. Finally, we must ask whether a true relationship develops between the supplier and the buyer as a result of both decision-making processes.

In order to cast some light on perception, decision-making, and, consequently, buying, we shall examine people's make-up and see what we can learn from psychology and behavioral analysis.

MAKING MARKETING DECISIONS

Imagine that you have to justify your annual marketing plan to the board of directors. You explain to them that you made an important decision by tossing a coin: heads for one option, tails for the other. It was tails, and that's why this is your plan. Your career will probably soon be over. So instead you tell a glowing story, throw in all sorts of figures to support your choice, and use arguments that play tactically on your colleagues' pet subjects, so that they are deluded into thinking that their own views are being taken fully into account. However your plan turns out, your career looks considerably brighter. If the results should take an unfavorable turn, you are the first to report it, with a plausible argument that the results are really not all that bad considering the circumstances, which are really nobody's fault at all. If you do this, you have little to fear. But is the intrinsic difference with the heads-or-tails option all that big?

If you really believe that human thought follows a clear and orderly sequence, you should take a look at the psychology of the human mind. Apparently the thought process can be described as a mess—for experts and nonexperts alike.[2] In fact, it is often the specialists who have confirmed convictions to which reasoning is subordinate. If you attend a seminar on new media, you will see that experts on both sides of the PC versus interactive cable TV issue do not have a shadow of a doubt about their positions. You will also notice that these experts cannot tolerate each other emotionally. So much for objective judgment.

People have a tendency to be prejudiced, and the conviction that we are right moves with the greatest ease through our nervous system. Information that contradicts what we believe is more difficult to accept than information that agrees with it; it's no fun having to reassess our opinions. Moreover, in a business situation we all have all sorts of interests in a certain judgment being accepted as the correct one: we want to try something different, we have trusted clients in the area concerned, we want to travel, or we see that, should the decision go the other way, our colleagues will take all the credit and we will bite the dust. In short, reasons enough to hunt down figures that fit in with our own priorities, and to play politics so that our colleagues do not take up arms against us.

But even if these interests are completely absent, questions have to be raised about the way people come to hold a certain point of view. We have a tendency to reach conclusions in an illogical and disorderly manner; information and logic are all too often neglected in matters that should be approached rationally. Jury decisions in criminal proceedings, especially in countries where the death penalty is imposed, sometimes provide chilling examples of how "legal and convincing evidence" overshadows the truth. Even within the field of psychology—that is, among people whose profession itself must alert them to the danger of illogical thinking—the problem can emerge in a clearly formulated and documented test situation.[3] So there is no reason to suppose that thought processes in marketing are any more orderly or logical than anywhere else. The heads-or-tails situation is thus a lot less crazy than it might first appear.

In consultative situations in which we are involved as marketing professionals, messy thinking can be recognized all too easily, especially regarding crucial strategic problems for which people ask our opinions. First we must understand what the real problem is for which the client requires advice. And that is by no means always the issue that is presented. Moreover, clients find it easier to think in solutions rather than in problems, so that we sometimes receive a vaguely phrased problem attached to a pretty concrete solution which the client expects us to evaluate. Because an external consultant has no vested interests or preferences, he can more easily give an unbiased judgment about the proposed solution than the parties involved. But then it first has to be very precisely established what the client's actual problem is. This is a skill in itself, because the picture is often distorted by parties in the client organization with vested interests.

At a later stage in the advisory process it is easy to see the considerable investment in time and thought that has to be made every time in order to establish whether the anticipated solution is the result of consistent reasoning. That is why, in our company, consultants who are not involved with the brief assess the advice, because they seem best able to judge whether a train of thought is unbiased. Those who realize how much difficulty the human brain, by its very nature, has with unbiased, consistent reasoning are no longer surprised by this continually recurring effort. That makes a difference.

Another factor that illustrates the brain's laborious process presents itself when the results of the advice do not agree with the desired advice. That requires the adviser to pay special attention to how they communicate their findings: arguments which do not agree with what the client had in mind seem to be particularly difficult to explain.

Behavioral psychology as well as recognizable experiences in the law and the profession of psychology itself make it clear that our thinking processes are chaotic, and that we can reach conclusions with the available information only in an illogical and disordered fashion. *The information revolution might well offer a staggering range of new possibilities, but the rationally deduced advantages will probably play only a limited role in decision making.* Will the type of decision making in organizations be altered by the information revolution? Are there tools—provided we allow them to enter into our decision-making process—that could compensate for the defective reasoning of our brains? In my judgment, an important step can be made here by organizations that seek to understand the possibilities. We shall return to this topic in Chapter 5.

MAKING PURCHASING DECISIONS

This brings us to the second question about human behavior that we must address in order to develop an insight into the new media: How do buyers reach their decisions? More precisely, what are people's perceptions of the media? How will people actively consult or passively experience the media to which they are exposed? And what bearing does this have on the practice of marketing via media? This type of marketing exists thanks to an understanding of its most definitive characteristic: a medium or information carrier. Since the process breaks down when the medium is incorrectly perceived or not noticed at all, our first question must be: How do people watch, read, and listen and what do people then appear to remember?

We start off by examining a few experiences with which most people are familiar, and to which they can relate. We then look at basic findings from the practice of marketing via media, and we again end by making a connection with psychology to clarify these experiences.

EXPERIENCES WE ALL RECOGNIZE

The notion that we experience everything around us to an approximately equal degree and without prejudice is, on the basis of our own observations, something we should dismiss. *Things that we see every day, year in and year out, turn out to be difficult to remember once they are no longer there.* Let's look at a few examples.

Imagine that every day we drive down a particular shopping street. We are so familiar with the street that we think we know every store on it. If one day a storefront disappears behind some anonymous boarding while renovations are carried out, we can barely remember which shop it was. In one test, a room full of people were asked to draw a picture of the dial of their watch without first looking at it. Few people were sure whether there were just dashes on the face to mark the hours or whether there were numbers and, if so, which. Yet we all look at our watches dozens of times each day. In another test, subjects were presented with crackers in a transparent wrapper clearly printed with the brand name; it turned out that none had noticed the brand. The only thing the subjects had apparently noticed, and made any associations with, were the crackers themselves. They noticed the brand name on the packaging only when the interviewer specifically drew their attention to it.

These examples all serve to illustrate how restricted our observations are. What we notice depends on a number of factors; if the familiar image of a shopping street changes, we can easily see that something is different, but we find it hard to pinpoint just what the change is. When we look to see what the time is, we barely notice whether the hands are pointing to dashes or figures, and if a package of crackers has caught our eye, we do not pay attention to what is printed on it. In none of these instances is there any question of bias. If there were, our perceptions would be even more distorted.

In Chapter 2, we saw what happens when people apply for a job with a well-known company or have a certain make of car brought to their attention. The moment we are drawn to a particular concern, we suddenly see its billboards, offices, or products everywhere. If we have developed an interest in a specific type of car, we start seeing it on the road far more often than we ever did before. This phenomenon, known as selective perception, illustrates the unreliability of reported information: We notice things more often not only when we encounter them more frequently, but also when our attention has previously been drawn to them.

Selective perception is of equal importance when addressing the question of how people perceive: If special or vested interests are introduced into the equation, our perception is once again affected. Further, that which we assume to be true appears to be distorted by moods or emotional baggage in the direction of our preferences and/or interests. Thus what we hear, expect, and describe—whether in political debates or football playoffs—is always biased in favor of the side we personally support. Similarly, if we are successful at something, we are likely to take credit for performing well. If we fail, despite considerable effort, we are likely to blame factors beyond our control. A familiar saying sums it up: "Failure is an orphan, but success has many fathers."

In an emotionally charged situation, with or without a particular interest in play, what we perceive to be true has even less to do with what has actually happened. Thus different eyewitnesses can, in all honesty, provide completely different accounts, sometimes—in cases where it is possible to establish the facts, such as by retrieving the "black box" in a plane crash—in total conflict with what must in reality have happened.[4] As previously stated, the information given by witnesses in these situations can be very unreliable. This is not because people are lying, but simply because they remember the event differently from the way it happened.

On the basis of these recognizable experiences, we obviously have to accept that what we make of all we see, read, and hear depends on numerous factors other than what is actually there. We can conclude that how we perceive things is highly subjective, and is based on what we know, our individual experiences, and our opinions. A knowledge of how people perceive is a prerequisite for using the media successfully to make transactions. Marketing depends on it.

Experiences from Direct Marketing

Once a medium (new or not) has been chosen after careful consideration, it must reach selected prospects that fit a marketing strategy. Let us start off by looking at a mailing, the classic and most common direct-marketing medium. Let us assume that the addressee is not a regular customer of the sender. In this case, in business markets as well as consumer markets, the medium is likely to be given only a cursory glance, and the receiver's primary response is to decide whether to throw it into the trash immediately or read it first. At a business address the mailing competes with other direct mail, with first-class letters, and with activities that are more important than sorting through the mail. The same largely holds true in the consumer market. The addressee gets home later than intended, is curious about the mail and sorts through it quickly, sometimes looking for a particular letter; what's more, dinner is getting cold. All in all, it is not an ideal time to read a mailing.

Even these highly unfavorable situations appear to be an adequate starting point for building a successful relationship between company and client, as long as the disadvantages are kept in mind. For safety's sake, it is best to assume that a mailing will be given very little attention, and that the receiver is determined to throw it away as quickly as possible. Put another way, as noted in Chapter 3, print media induce action, even if it is just to throw the mailing away.

If the sender is a familiar name or a regular supplier of the prospect, the mailing is likely to receive more attention. People always open letters from their bank or insurance company. The contents won't be read with the same attention as a letter from a long-lost friend, but will be skimmed to see if there are any points of interest. People give mailings from unknown senders about as much attention as they pay to the headlines when glancing through the newspaper. And, of course, the closer the contents lie to the interests of the prospects, the greater the chance of catching their attention.

There is a certain order, independent of our preferences, in the way we perceive various stimuli presented to us. If a marketing medium contains text and illustrations, we are first drawn to the illustrations. If these images are of objects and people, we first look at the people; if they are only of people, we first look at the eyes. The first things we notice when looking at a piece of text are the heading and signature, and, if there is one, the postscript. Next come the words that have a personal significance for us: name, address, ID number, employer, names of family members, date of birth, and so on. Following this come the ordinary words, of which short words with a positive tone work best—*yes, good, fast, free*—but also *breakthrough, result, solution.* Negative words run the risk of eliciting negative associations: *none, never, danger, problems, price increase.* It is therefore essential to avoid double negatives if you have something positive to say.

For example, every year around Christmas, you receive a letter from your supplier informing you of a price increase. This year is no exception. At first glance you know what the letter is about: a price increase. The letter, with its assumed contents, is quickly skimmed through and the expected words "price increase" indeed appear, confirming your expectations. The fact that this time the word "no" appears before "price increase" is something that you and other readers may not notice. Whoever rereads the letter, noticing the "no" this time, develops a second negative association. So, the sender runs the risk of creating two negative associations for a positive message. "Another wretched price increase," thinks the reader at first, and then goes on to complain: "And it's not even true!"

In mail-order operations, it is important to gain insight as quickly as possible into the distribution of demand for articles in a product range. One of the methods used by the Dutch brand of Great Universal Stores was to invite regular clients to a meeting where a mock-up of the new catalog was presented. In this way, even before the actual catalog appeared, the selected clients could provide an idea of the demand for various items in the collection; the mail-order company could then adjust its orders to its own suppliers. One problem was that a large number of clients associated this type of invitation from this particular mail-order company with a fashion show, and were disappointed.

To avoid a repeat of the problem, the text for the next series of invitations was changed. The company explained far more clearly that people were being invited to look at the mock-up pages of the catalog and stated that "therefore it is not a fashion show." The result was that the number of complaints grew. What's more some clients complained that the invitation had clearly stated that there would be a fashion show. The same principle is at work here as in the "price increase" example cited earlier. People expected a fashion show; in glancing through the invitation they saw the expected words "fashion show" and didn't notice the word "not" preceding it. As a result the gatherings were abandoned, and other methods were found to evaluate the demand for the items in the catalog.

The order in which we perceive things can be summarized as follows:

- Images of people's eyes
- Images of people
- Images of objects
- Headline, signature, postscript
- Text containing recipient's name and familiar numbers
- Short, positive words

These are all elements that help attract the attention of the addressee within the few seconds it takes to decide whether to throw the mailing in the trash. Elements that usually confuse readers are abstract concepts (words ending, for example, in -*ness*), long words, and technical jargon that nobody understands. These words are overlooked, work against (as do negative words) a positive attitude, or are simply forgotten; we cannot remember that which we do not understand. In contrast, pictorial concepts stick in our memories.

For example, it is almost impossible for adults to reproduce a sentence in a foreign language with which they are completely unacquainted. People cannot associate images with the unfamiliar sounds. The sounds become recognizable only when the individual words and the overall structure of the sentence have been explained. On a map of Beijing, Western visitors may have difficulty distinguishing between the often long street names; what's more, these names change slightly every few kilometers, and Westerners have to look very carefully in order to spot the difference. If a visitor knows a handful of words in Chinese, these same names, which were hardly distinguishable at first, are suddenly far more recognizable; they are then easier to distinguish and memorize. Take, for example, "Avenue of the Revolution in front of the gate" and "Avenue of the Revolution behind the gate"; understanding the words "Revolution," "in front of," "behind," and "gate" makes everything clear.

The dominance of visual stimuli has important implications for the design of media. The first superficial observations, which must lead to closer examination of the content rather than a decision to throw something away, are apparently determined by the image. The text can reinforce that image but hardly alter it. Put another way: If there is a picture of a dog, and the text warns the reader against thinking of a dog, you can be sure that if the reader thinks of anything, it will be a dog. In thematic advertising campaigns, where it can hardly be established which images are retained and with what associations, this mistake is made frequently. There is no direct feedback. In direct marketing, or with media in their advanced uses, the feedback is instantaneous and any incorrect associations are immediately uncovered.

During a discussion on this subject on a television program, I was asked to give an example. Right then I remembered a commercial for Skoda that began "Cars from the Eastern bloc rust..." and a couple of other commonly held negative views. The voice-over said: "But this car is designed by Bertone..." or words to that effect. The perceptual progression is as follows: The negative statements are recognizable and familiar, so they are easily accepted by the viewer's nervous system as an affirmation of previously accepted ideas. Thus the negative prejudices of the viewer are flatly confirmed by the commercial. The statement "But this car is designed by Bertone" runs two risks: Either viewers do not realize that Bertone is a famous designer—which, by the way, is no guarantee against rust—or they do know Bertone, in which case the claim is so implausible that the risk of rejection by the nervous system is considerable.

It goes without saying that after citing this example on TV I got a letter from the advertising agency stating that a new campaign had been launched and that my criticism was not much appreciated. Rightly so. Because I do not want to alienate all my potential customers, I wrote a friendly letter back asking to see something from the new campaign—of which I had no recollection—in the hope of being able to make some favorable comment. I received my answer. The new campaign was enclosed. I had in fact seen it, but I had not realized that it was an advertisement for Skoda. But this was a good thing too:

The ad shows a dejected driver, vainly trying to get help using a broken emergency phone draped in cobwebs. There is a car in the background, apparently a Skoda. In effect the copy says that if emergency phones were there only for Skoda drivers, they would all be covered in cobwebs and out of service, because Skodas never break down. The advertisement was potentially more disastrous than the previous one. It ran the considerable risk of linking Skodas with emergency phones, breakdowns, and unsuccessful attempts to get help on the one hand—all unpleasant associations. And this is precisely the connection that was not intended. The copy was powerless to explain away the negative imagery. The only hope for the advertisement was that nobody would recognize the car as a Skoda.

Once a direct-mail campaign catches the reader's attention, it should develop a line of reasoning similar to that used by a salesperson. Vögele[5] recommends viewing a mailing as a dialogue in which the questions commonly raised by prospective customers are answered positively. A useful sequence is:

- Who is writing to me
- Why
- What is being offered
- Who demonstrates this
- What I must do

The AIDA acronym for one-to-one selling can be superimposed on this sequence directly:

- *Attention* (who is writing to me)
- *Interest* (why)
- *Desire* (what is being offered, who demonstrates this)
- *Action* (what I must do)

The reader needs only to nod in agreement at each step, as it were, in order to consent to move through the selling process.

Academicians who scrutinize a mailing with the thoroughness reserved for a scientific treatise will conclude that it was written with the lowest common denominator of the public. But this need not concern us here. As already mentioned, most direct-mail recipients dedicate only a very limited amount of their intelligence to understanding the mailing; intelligent people should also be able to assess, at a glance, whether there is something of interest in the mailing. This is why reply coupons are written in clear and large lettering- "FILL IN, CUT OUT, SEND IN"—preferably with a pair of scissors pointing out the dotted line. This must not be mistaken for instructions on how to use the coupon, but to make it clear to the addressee who is casually glancing at it that something needs to be sent in.

In summary, in order to use media to accomplish a sale, we need to adhere to certain guidelines based on how people perceive, read, listen, and remember. There are no hard-and-fast rules for success, but avoidable risks can be clearly established. A learning process is created by the direct feedback between the message and its outcome.

EXPERIENCES FROM ADVERTISING RESEARCH

There is generally no direct feedback on the outcome of advertising. Furthermore, the "result" is usually measured, not in sales, but in coverage, awareness, and stated product preference. Because taste can also play a role in what the public finds appealing or creative, many subjective factors come into play over which advertisers have very little control.

Since Walter Scott published *The Theory of Advertising*[6] in 1903, various aspects of this subject have been researched. In Germany especially a fair amount of scientific research has been conducted into what requirements an advertisement must fulfill in order to be seen, understood, and remembered as quickly as possible. Typically, subjects are shown advertisements and are then asked what they have seen and understood. In addition, a specialized apparatus has been used to plot the physical movements of the eye and what the eye observes. There are also methods to measure changes in the body's electrical impulses, whereby the intensity of the elicited response on the nervous system (but not whether it is positive or negative) can be plotted. The results show many parallels with knowledge accumulated in the field of direct marketing. It is all a lot more complex than merely counting how many people have sent in a coupon, but these sorts of methods provide very useful guidelines for effective advertising. In fact, these guidelines concern everything that we perceive and that grabs our attention. It is therefore a question of universal human perception, independent of goal or medium, so the results are also important for the new marketing era.

One of the prerequisite goals of advertising is to attract the attention of intended target groups. Gundolf Meyer-Hensche[7] identifies three types of stimuli that establish the attention value of advertisements and that, in my opinion, are of equal importance in other applications:

- Emotional stimuli
- Intellectual stimuli
- Physical stimuli

Emotional stimuli are part of the classic repertoire of attention-getting devices. That is understandable, because they are rooted in our psyche. They make us flee at the threat of danger, or explore something that arouses our curiosity. We react to these basic instincts reflexively, and have no power to control the involuntary response they evoke. Whoever succeeds in arousing these emotions is guaranteed a reaction. Erotic stimuli are the strongest, but in advertising they must in some way relate to the product; otherwise the connection escapes the viewer's attention and the stimuli work as a distraction. The irresistible emotional stimuli that are communicated by the face, something familiar to the world of direct marketing, are also powerful.[8]

Intellectual stimuli can be generated using images as well as words. They cause us to frown because a statement is controversial or illogical—imagine someone wearing a winter coat on a palm-fringed beach. Here, though, the risk of negative associations is introduced.

Physical stimuli are also well known in the world of direct marketing. They are used excessively, for example, in mail-order catalogs.[9] The manipulation of bright colors, image size, and contrast, and how compellingly the copy is presented, are all determining factors. Thus, on the back of a mail-order catalog, the copy jumps at you from the page. Using too many small elements in one photo can make the visual too confusing. One large, compelling element commands attention. These too are elements to which a person forcefully and unconsciously responds, because these reflexes are located in the oldest parts of the human nervous system. Our reaction to the color red, as a signal of danger, also fits in here. *Traffic lights and emergency switches in cars are red for a very good reason.* In advertising, these same elements are used to attract attention, even though the color red has little to do with blood, as it did in our distant past. Our nervous system has not yet forgotten the connection.

In the advertising world, according to Meyer-Hentschel, we first notice the image, then the form, and finally the content, particularly with regard to the attention value of headlines. Words that arouse emotion are effective only if they can be read at a glance. Advertising needs to be very careful when playing on words, if the desired result is to attract attention. Most wordplay is too cumbersome to be understood at a glance. Time and again tests show that the human eye is distracted by the smallest detail. A wonderful background for the presentation of ad copy can easily overshadow the copy itself. In principle, the same holds true for journals and books: Text superimposed on an equally striking background is far less easy to read. And then people don't bother to read it. David Ogilvy observed all this as early as 1964.[10] Haven't we learned anything from his findings?

Meyer-Hentschel tested six motives to establish which had the highest attention value, which had the lowest, and the order of those in between. The test group consisted of 136 women between the ages of 20 and 49. The tests were conducted with the aid of electronic equipment and thus did not rely on stated answers. The resulting ranking showed a clear order of the pictures: no doubt the picture just showing eyes ranked first, next was the picture with a complete human face, followed by the picture of a cat, the picture of an unusual object, one of a normal object, and one of some dull hardly visible tiles.

Up to now a few insights from the field of advertising research have been discussed which, although coming from a different standpoint from that of direct marketing, show perfectly analogous results. I see no reason to suppose that these findings cannot, in an appropriately adapted form, be applied to new media.

PERCEPTIONS FROM NEW MEDIA

The preconditions discussed up to now have been based on experiences with print media and with radio and TV commercials. The new media demand a new interpretation, attuned to each medium itself. Here, just as in direct marketing, we can learn what the effects of various presentations are through direct feedback. The same preconditions apply as in the existing media.

Voice-Response Computer.   My experience with the development of voice-response dialogues suggests that they do not differ much from traditional media. However, they do provide additional insights into physical (auditory) stimuli.

1. The auditory experience via an automatic system is extremely *transient*; in any case, it is far more short-lived than via print media, which can be consulted more than once. Listeners can repeat a voice dialogue by pressing a phone button, but few people make use of this facility. The text therefore has to be clear in one go. On the other hand, contrary to most other applications, it is the prospect who takes the initiative to make the phone call and is therefore more inclined to listen.

2. Depending on the degree of familiarity with and the content of the dialogue, we must be prepared for the fact that

the prospect experiences a computer-generated voice as providing *less certainty* than a signed letter. If only information is being provided, this isn't really a problem, as long as the information is understood correctly. But if a transaction is being conducted, the dialogue's text and tone must leave the client no room for hesitation. When using the telephone voice-response ordering service of a leading European mail-order company, customers were initially inclined to double-check the transaction by using the "live" conventional order phone to find out if "the order had in fact been registered." Unfortunately, in the initial stages the system did not allow orders to be verified immediately, so the customer often placed the order a second time just to be sure. The problem was solved by adding a confirmatory sentence after each order—"Your order has been noted"—spoken with such conviction that nobody was left with a shadow of doubt. Another possibility—sending confirmation of an order via fax—can be used to excellent effect, particularly in the business market.

3. A company is often unaware that the dialogue needs *precision.* Whereas in a mailing, all sorts of departments, up to and including top management, wish to see the contents beforehand, the voice dialogue is often made mechanically, as part of the project. What's more, the dialogue may be seen primarily as an automation project, calling for different emphasis than in a marketing project. The process is, as it were, too technically directed. Companies that sell voice-response systems, despite their experience, are not marketers for their customers.

4. The *choice of words* in a voice-response dialogue tends to be the same as that used internally in a business context. In a brochure, the choice of words is corrected by the advertising agency, but this attention to detail for a voice dialogue is often missing. Further, since a voice-response dialogue is by nature transitory, any inaccuracies can cause the whole process to fail. We checked the dialogue for a Dutch car-leasing company. Right from the start, the caller was presented with a choice between a car and a van. Unfortunately the

Dutch word that professional sellers use for "van" is the same word that consumers use for "company car." Many callers wanted a car that would be paid for by the company— and would therefore be a company car—and they became so confused that the whole process broke down. Our client had used the vocabulary of the seller rather than of the buyer. If callers are confused, particularly early on in the dialogue, they will almost certainly terminate the call. Correction of these sorts of details by adapting the vocabulary to the customer's spoken language is a prerequisite for success.

5. Auditory perceptions generate more *limited recall* than visual perceptions. The number of possible choices confronting a caller needs to be limited; otherwise the caller will become confused. A maximum of five possibilities is a good guideline. Likewise, a caller must not be required to make too many choices before hearing the required information. *People lose track of auditory information far more easily than visual information.* Therefore the "conversation" should not be so long as to run the risk of irritating the caller.

DRTV, Infomercials, and TV Shopping.   A second range of media that is on the rise consists of direct-response TV, infomercials, and home shopping channels. DRTV, as one of the first and simplest forms of interactivity via that medium, offers direct feedback for clearly establishing what causes the viewer to respond in the desired manner. The results are not very encouraging for those with a penchant for artistic style. On the other hand, vendors recognize the findings all too well.

The objective of a DRTV commercial is to get unsuspecting viewers out of their chairs to make a phone call, in just a short space of time. The viewer may be invited to gain more information or to place an order, but it is always a "call to action."

The amount of time available to get the viewer to act differs substantially depending on the type of advertisement. DRTV commercials run for somewhere between 30 and 60 seconds. Infomercials last a lot longer, up to 30 or 40 minutes, but they make use of the same principles to persuade viewers to respond. Finally, there are companies that devote themselves exclusively to this type of broadcast, such as QVC and the Home Shopping Network. These run 24 hours a day, changing the advertised goods as necessary. Although there are many differences among these three forms, there are nevertheless significant similarities in the way they seek to get the viewer to act. All three rely on the basic principles of human perception that must be adhered to if the medium is to be used successfully. These preconditions concern the product, the special offer, and the invitation to purchase or "call to action."

1. *The product.* There should be absolutely no confusion about what product is being advertised. It must be convincingly and permanently visible without giving rise to any misunderstanding. "What's in it for me?" must be clear to the viewer the whole way through, thereby playing on primal emotions. Frequently recurring themes are health, comfort, and happiness. The visual portrayal of these themes works best. The home shopping channels further emphasize these themes by letting viewers hear testimonials from buyers who are much happier and healthier since purchasing the displayed product.

2. *The special offer.* Important elements are the (special) price, the exclusivity of the offer (where possible "not available at any store"), and the no-risk nature of the order—for example, "satisfaction guaranteed—or your money back." Any perceived risk must be considered negligible, and the uniqueness of the opportunity must be emphasized.

3. *The purchase invitation.* This is simply the "Call now!" message, during which time the telephone number must be clearly presented. People stop seeing something if it is permanently visible, so it is better to have the number fade in and out several times.

A good response sometimes depends on the most peculiar details. American infomercials that are shown in Europe are often "badly" dubbed—just out of step with the mouth movements in the original language. I asked one of my clients, responsible for these infomercials, if they could be synchronized better to be less irritating. I should have known the answer. Whenever the films were synchronized more precisely, as they had been several times because of the client's own annoyance, sales fell dramatically. Obviously the impact of an infomercial is greater if sound and movement are just out of step, so they are deliberately dubbed in this way.

When a direct-response TV advertisement is longer than a standard commercial, the key aspects for success are that it be amusing, communicative, and informative, and that it offers the opportunity to respond. As we will see, the same applies to the new media. It is helpful to compare direct-response television with a salesperson selling kitchen knives at a home appliances fair. The form and technique have changed, but the basic pitch is the same. People continue to be susceptible to the same primary stimuli.

New Media in General.   The more senses that can be stimulated and the more effectively this is achieved, the stronger the perception of the stimuli. Full-screen motion video with sound is the ultimate form, in combination with a high degree of individuality and interactivity.

Behavioral psychology has clearly shown that our senses are interrelated. A condition for success with multimedia, therefore, is to balance sound and image carefully to achieve the desired effect. Music and images are remembered more easily if they bear a clear relationship to each other. Different images, and particularly different colors, create a different perception of the same piece of music. Just how much the senses interrelate can be illustrated by the well-known experiment in which potatoes turned blue under certain lighting, causing people to find their flavor disagreeable.

Because people are inclined to remember in images, new media with a visual component have the possibilities. The human memory is less efficient at retaining unrelated trivia than interconnected events. A commonly used technique for remembering is association. Events that we have forgotten and all the associations linked with them, resurface when we find ourselves in a similar situation. In order to use the new media successfully, it is important to work visually and to present the images in a structured way so that viewers can understand and remember them better.

An extremely critical element of new media, and one for which the philosopher's stone remains to be discovered, is the method by which people make a choice from the many possibilities on offer. It is the problem of finding software that requires no instruction manual. In numerous trials with the new interactive media carried out in the United States, four components emerged as essential for success.

1. *Entertainment.*   People first and foremost want to be entertained, whatever the medium.

2. *Communication.*   There should always be some form of communication, either between medium and receiver, or between different people who can be distinguished on the medium; human interest, and the experiences of customers with the product, are part of this. "Since I gave this product to my friends as a gift, we have become better friends" is an example.

3. *Transaction.*   The public must be able to perform a transaction: request information, order, join in a game, or give opinions.

4. *Information.*   "Just look at the possibilities, all available in three colors." Product information is of great importance.

The tests relied on panels of users. It became evident that what people most wanted was more information so they could use the systems more frequently. But the addition of more information did not increase the use in any way. Then, games were added without being requested. The result: the level of use increased. This illustrates precisely how the human nervous system works: Simple temptations are far more effective than intellectual reasoning.

In summary, knowledge of how the media are perceived should form the primary and most important background for anyone involved with the new media. Voice-response communication and DRTV are an integral part of this, adding their own set of characteristics. From the viewpoint of behavioral psychology there are additional facts that are of primary importance in the perception of new media. *A lot of time and money are spent rediscovering things that are already known about existing media in marketing functions and that behavioral psychologists regard as elementary knowledge.* A new medium can add new properties that need to be taken into account from the point of view of perception; but these are valid in addition to what is already known. The trials can be limited to these additions—a difficult enough task. New media experts who claim that everything connected with new media is new are demonstrating their own ignorance.

BEHAVIORAL PSYCHOLOGY AND ERGONOMICS

Basic tenets of behavioral psychology, research into the new media, and experience with the media themselves suggest that we are not just groping in the dark in the new marketing era. If suppliers have a better understanding of how different media are perceived, they can anticipate the prospect's reaction by choosing the appropriate medium and its production. The chance of achieving favorable results increases dramatically.

PEOPLE HAVE BEEN PREPROGRAMMED

Up to now our focus has largely been on the empirical facts that apply to Western society—independent of country or language, market or product. In this sense they are universally valid; they are an inherent part of the human phenomenon. To gain some understanding of why people seem to react in this way, and thus to be better equipped to predict patterns of response, a basic understanding of behavioral psychology can be useful. This section elucidates some of the underlying ideas of behavioral psychology.

Special characteristics of human perception, communication, and behavior are dependent on how people are constructed biologically. The general principle can be illustrated with animals: An animal that can fly must be equipped with wings. An animal with long legs can take long strides. An animal with two eyes and an overlapping field of vision can judge distances. Rabbits do not have an overlapping field of vision and cannot judge distances, but they do have a very wide field of vision whereby they can see danger on all sides and without the need to judge distances can take to their heels. The perception of depth depends not only on the overlapping position of the eyes, but also on shadows and perspective.

Psychological processes are also influenced by physical factors. "A full stomach is not good for study." That is what our biology teacher told us, implying that if our blood is needed for digestion there is less left over for the brain's processes. Another physical factor that appears to influence psychological processes is our posture. People seem to be more alert and quicker to react when standing than when seated. *For that reason alone, it is worthwhile holding meetings with people on their feet; it saves a lot of time.* Up to now, the connection with direct marketing probably seems rather remote. But such evolutionary physical characteristics are particularly interesting because of their effect on human behavior, including people's buying behavior via the media. They are therefore an essential point to consider in marketing.

The pace of modern life makes it especially important that information be presented in a clear and obvious manner. Thus the intention of a direct-response advertisement must be immediately clear. And if the information is relevant to prospects, they must immediately be able to react appropriately. People do not have the time to think these things over, or do not take the time. On the highway, larger-than-life traffic signs, fluorescent warnings of imminent danger, flashing lights, and speed bumps all try to ensure that drivers remain safely on the right track. If a traffic situation changes from what drivers are accustomed to, even more signs are posted to warn of these changes. A construction detour may be clearly visible and adequately signposted, but special boards will be put up half a mile before it to remind people of what's ahead. Otherwise, people will stick to the driving patterns they were accustomed to before the detour was created. Then the awakening comes as a double blow.

Despite all the attention given to this matter, signposts do not always provide essential information in a way that is immediately comprehensible. If you ever happen to be driving in Holland, watch out as you approach the loop around Amsterdam. *Nobody has been able to explain to me why you have to follow the signs directing you to the east of Amsterdam when you know for a fact that you want to go west. Perhaps the experts know better.* But we drivers are totally confused. The first time you may take a gamble—and it turns out to be wrong. So the next time you know that if you want to go west, then you have to follow the signs directing you east!

On one of the highways that leads to a tunnel under the North Sea Canal, I once noticed that just before the tunnel other drivers were irresponsibly cutting into my lane, while gesturing furiously to me. For my own peace of mind I put this down to paranoia, until one day my wife pointed out that I was driving through a red light just before the tunnel. The confusion had arisen as a result of a combination of roadwork in the tunnel and the traffic density, and green arrows directed drivers to the appropriate traffic lanes. Among these green arrows, there was sometimes a round green light, depending on how busy it was at the time. If there was a green light, it could also turn red: traffic lights. In all my years of driving this route I had never noticed them. The following time I searched carefully between the green arrows for those circles. It was only then I realized that the big warning signs in the middle of the lane showed these traffic lights. If there was a light among the arrows, the signs would flash. But not otherwise. Perhaps the lights should have sunk into the ground when they weren't in use, because for me they had just become a normal feature, flashing or not. And this meant I just didn't notice them.

ERGONOMICS AND MARKETING

Ergonomics deals with the physical and psychological factors that determine how people can best use all sorts of equipment. Initially, ergonomics was mainly concerned with the workplace, but now it is applied in all kinds of situations.

Ergonomics plays an important role in the design of instrument panels, tools, and train and aircraft interiors. Instrument panels have to be easily understood, especially in the event of an emergency. The button for the emergency lights has to be found without an exhaustive study of the instruction manual. In my first Audi, the alarm button could be found in an instant, but it was exactly the same shape as the button that switched off the ABS (antilock brake system); what's more, the buttons were right next to each other. We know that in a panic situation our fine motor controls work less accurately, so on the rare occasion of an emergency stop I often accidentally hit the button that disables the ABS at the same time as hitting the alarm button. Exactly in a situation when I needed this brake computer, I may have disabled it! This design blunder seems to have been solved by completely removing the ABS button.

Tools and household appliances also have to be used almost automatically in the correct way. A new appliance is usually so attractive that you want to use it as soon as possible, without wading through all the literature. If there is a large, inviting knob on the new gadget, that will be the first thing that is pulled or pushed, depending on which way it moves most easily. It is the designer's job to ensure that the machine does exactly what the user expects. Only when pushing and pulling the buttons doesn't get the expected result will the owner consult the instruction manual. Designers tried to improve the ergonomic quality of the mouse on my PC by integrating it into the keyboard. Both mouse buttons are now found at the front of the keyboard, where I place the palms of my hands while typing. Initially this led to disaster, because totally incomprehensible pictures would appear on my screen at the most unexpected moments. Now it is apparent that the palm of my hand had probably touched one of the two mouse buttons. But it's still a matter of trial and error.

The interior of the train through the tunnel under the English Channel between France and England is designed to avoid even the slightest hint of claustrophobia under all circumstances. The interiors of the Airbus and the Boeing 767 are designed to create the impression of being in a comfortable space. And a shop interior can be designed so that the client feels comfortable and buys as much as possible.

A well-known ergonomic problem is designing automatic dispensing machines to serve people better. Quality of service is not so important if there are specific reasons for taking refuge in a machine. For example, your bank may be closed after normal business hours. Or you may not want to run the risk, during regular hours, that someone half your age will present you with embarrassing information about your balance as you try to withdraw money. In both cases, a cash machine is the ideal solution.

We have now entered the realm of economic transactions. The appearance of all aspects of a vending machine can determine to a large extent whether people use it to buy tickets, to end up getting a snack that they didn't even intend to buy, or to take a chance on a one-armed bandit. If we regard the machine as the medium, then it is in fact a case of direct marketing. Seen in this way, ergonomics is actually closer to direct marketing than may at first appear. Aspects of ergonomics also play an important role in situations where people find themselves in a potential purchasing position, such as in shops and standing in front of shelves full of products. The comparison with billboards and other forms of communication that potentially attract people to make a purchase is very clear. *Behavioral psychology and ergonomics reveal part of the programming according to which people seem to react.* It is thus important for marketers to follow the work of those who are involved with these professional fields, whether operationally, scientifically, or in an advisory capacity.

THE CONSTRUCTION OF THE BRAIN AND ITS SIGNIFICANCE FOR MARKETING

In the same way that the structure of the body's bones and muscles are important for physical skills, the construction of the brain plays a critical role in the process of observation. Experts in behavioral psychology and in neurology emphasize different aspects of how perceptions are formed. We will examine a few of these differences.

FROM STIMULATION TO ACTION

Although smell and taste are of vital importance to animals, humans are primarily regarded as visual creatures. The senses of smell and taste have certainly not been lost in the course of evolution, and their significance should not be underestimated, but our vision of the world is primarily constructed from the light waves that enter through the lenses of our eyes and are turned into images by a highly complex process. For the nonpsychologist, the processes of observation are shown diagrammatically in Fig. 4-1.

The medium generates the stimulation that the senses receive and that subsequently travels to the brain, where all sorts of judgments and preconceptions about reality exist. Incoming experiences are reshaped by these preformed intellectual constructions, to create a meaningful perception that can lead to action. In spite of the oversimplification, it is clear that the same sensory stimuli can give rise to differing meaningful perceptions, depending on what is already in our minds. In Chapter 2 we saw how different people, in response to the same observation—for instance, the perceptions of salespeople about their chances in the market—can, in all truthfulness, reach totally different conclusions and as a result act very differently.

Consider the story of two shoe sellers who visit a tropical island. One returns full of enthusiasm, reporting that there is

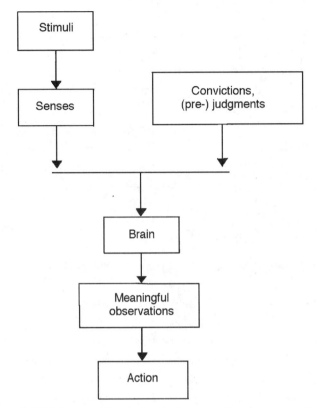

FIGURE 4-1.   From stimulation to action.

a fantastic market for shoes "because nobody has shoes yet." The second representative returns completely discouraged, saying that there is no market for shoes whatsoever "because nobody buys shoes." Apart from the shoe sellers' ignorance of the African continent, the story demonstrates the difference between optimism and caution. As a result of differing emotional makeup, and the resulting prejudices, the same information leads to very different courses of action.

The debate arises as to whether people trade on the basis of their information or trade on the basis of emotional influences and then look for the information that justifies it. In my view, behavior is just as likely to arise from emotional reasons as from rational ones, depending on the situation in which people find themselves. In neither case does information have to lead to uniform behavior. The complicated coupling between perception and behavior emphasizes the importance of direct feedback on the effect of the communication.[11] Via feedback, you can find the actual actions made on the grounds of the impulse generated by a medium. In fact, you can bypass the discussions within the psychological sciences: You simply establish what has actually happened and which changes in the impulses lead to which changes in response. Thus the result can be optimized step by step, without accurate knowledge of the hidden psychological processes.

TWO WAYS TO UNDERSTAND THE BRAIN

The manager or marketer who takes the trouble to wrestle through a number of basic ideas of neurology will reach some surprising conclusions. If you still have any hesitations about the usefulness of database marketing for commercial strategy, you should take a look at the structure of the human brain.

There are two generally accepted theories of how the brain is organized. The first is an arrangement of patterns of behavioral specialization and neural areas of association, adapted from Mesulam.[12] The second is an arrangement that shows the age in evolutionary terms of each specific brain area and the essential functions that are principally controlled by them. The first arrangement is generally used in neurology and concentrates on architectonic structure and neural connections. The second emphasizes output as the most important factor and is closer to behavioral psychology; according to many neurologists, it uses models that are obsolete and too general. The first arrangement focuses attention on the connections and their complexity, while the second concentrates precisely on the lack of coordination between output from the different systems. In this sense, it is difficult to compare the two models. Both approaches shed a surprising new light on human perception and on its consequences for marketing and market research.

The first arrangement, shown in Figure 4-2, classifies different zones in the human brain depending on their proximity to the external world ("extrapersonal space") and the human internal world ("internal milieu"). The classification allows us to deduce general principles about the organization of associative patterns as well as behavioral specializations.

The sensory and motor regions are closest to the external world. These parts of the cortex convey the sensory input from the surroundings and coordinate the actions that lead to the manipulation of the extrapersonal space. The primary visual, auditory, and other perceptions through the senses are based here. The neighboring unimodal cortex provides the neural machinery for the subsequent processing of sensory input. In the heteromodal cortex, according to this view, the different modalities (sight, hearing, and so on) are combined into one single perception. There is thus already an obvious hierarchy that can be seen in the processing of sensory stimuli. Even the differentiation between sensory and motor input is no longer present. It could be argued that during the process of perception, the senses are not passive doorways where the input

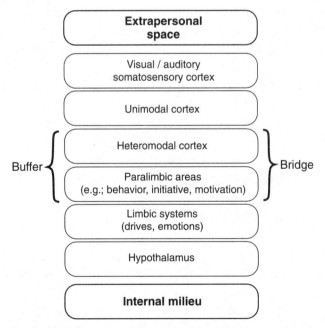

FIGURE 4-2. Zones in the human brain, arranged between the external and internal world.

streams in, but are actively scanning tentacles. The building blocks of perception are just as much the motor as the sensory phenomena themselves, as is clearly shown physiologically in these heteromodal areas.

There are thus at least two essential transformations that take place in the neural regions:

1. Associations are built up from different sensory modalities, as required by many cognitive processes, especially for language.
2. There is interaction between fully processed sensory information and input from other structures, including the limbic system.

This heteromodal cortex and the uppermost layer of the limbic system form a bridge as well as a buffer. In this sense, the inner and outer worlds converge at this point.

The limbic system makes it clear how emotions and drives that originate in the inner milieu can influence the way in which people perceive themselves and the world, and how thoughts and experiences can influence emotions.

The hypothalamus is closest to the human inner milieu. It manages important elementary functions, including the body's temperature, the blood sugar levels, and blood pressure, through hormonal and neural mechanisms. Directly above the hypothalamus is the limbic system, which is closely tied to these functions of the hypothalamus and which is assumed to play an important role in memory, learning, passions, and emotions. These specialized functions of the limbic system are closely related to the internal milieu and to the necessary activities that ensure the continuation of the species. In the "higher," paralimbic areas, components such as behavior, initiative, motivation, and planning are processed.

The uppermost layers of the limbic system and the heteromodal cortex coming from the outside world form a neural bridge (as well as buffer) between the needs of the inner milieu and the reality of the external milieu. This confrontation enables the brain to go in search of further associations in the processing of sensory perceptions, and also makes it possible to integrate the information with emotions and passions.

From the above, it can once again be deduced that the same stimuli—a mailing, for example—can lead to totally different perceptions and reactions, as much dependent on the person who perceives them as on the conditions that are generated by their internal milieu. The trick is to generate as many positive associations as possible with a medium, given the structures of the human brain. As noted earlier, research can show how best to stimulate these positive associations in the human brain. Similarly, research suggests that completely different connections in the brain are operating when people take action than when people offer their opinion without taking action. The difference may depend, among other things, on disposition or temper—something that we can easily recognize in ourselves. The important distinction between intended and actual behavior, as mentioned before, can hardly surprise us if we consider it from a neurological point of view.

The second arrangement of the brain is also a help in understanding the heuristic model, even though it is less accurate and tricky to compare with the first. This second arrangement, shown in Figure 4-3, is a classification according to the age in evolutionary terms of the different brain sys-

Brain type	Evolutionary Age	Essential Functions
Hypothalamus, small brain	500 million years old	Addiction, instinctive reflexes, behavior (reptile)
Limbic system	200 million years old	Emotions, fight, flight, complex actions (mammals)
Neocortex	0.1 million years old, with a spurt of growth	Symbolic information, memory, use of language, reasoning, intellect, contemplation (humans)

FIGURE 4-3.   Types of brain systems according to evolutionary age and function.

tems and according to the essential functions for which they seem primarily responsible. There are opposing theories about the relationships among the different brain systems, but the finer points are not of great importance to the marketing professional.

In the age-based classification, the neocortex is the archetypal human brain and is a very recent evolutionary development. It has been ascertained that the brain has experienced a spurt of growth over the last 50,000 years. The last anatomical changes were even more recent—about 35,000 years ago. This is the period that Homo sapiens, such as the Cro-Magnon people, started to populate Europe. But not much has changed since then. Functions of the typical human neocortex are concerned with the ability to form abstractions, the ego, the self, and *thinking*. In short, this is a computer that manages what we think and say.

In this arrangement, the limbic system is primarily associated with complex, integrated behavior, and is essential for the expression of passions and emotions. The limbic system is highly developed in mammals, and in this context it controls people's and animals' *actions*. If the neocortex is the computer that controls what we say, the limbic system is the computer that controls what we do.

The third and oldest computer, the brain stem, controls vital functions such as heartbeat, breathing, swallowing, eye movements, and digestion. The hypothalamus controls factors such as mood, hunger, and thirst. The small brains take care of the coordination and modulation of movement. All these functions are primarily unconscious and are difficult to control. The oldest computer is responsible for what we cannot help doing. Reptiles do not have much more than this operating system.

Vroon [13] questions the relative autonomy of these three systems, whereas neurology specialists examine the interconnectivity and the important channeling functions. Instead of emphasizing the limited degree to which the three systems communicate with each other, we could also argue that they do not always communicate adequately, and sometimes run amok. We can all fall victim to moods and emotions that we neither want to experience nor understand, and in certain situations we can do things that in hindsight make us wonder how the situation got so out of hand. *The three different systems are like computers of three very different generations and barely communicate with each other.* In this context, it is essential to recognize that in human (as opposed to animal) behavior, remarkable contradictions can arise.

For example, our "human brain" can offer explanations that cannot be faulted in any way. We can explain our understanding of a particular message and then state what we think about it and what we plan to do. Then we can go and behave according to our "mammalian brains," in a way that is utterly contradictory with what we have just sincerely argued. We know that fatty foods and gluttony are harmful for our health, that smoking is bad for our own and other people's health—it is even written in big letters on the packet—and that driving fast is damaging for the environment. Our neocortex makes us understand all that, but then our limbic system lets us eat too much, smoke, and drive like mad. *In short, we love healthy food, but not at mealtimes.* In the same way, the impact of concern with the environment on people's behavior is still hardly as significant as we would imagine from the opinions expressed in the research.

In fact, these same contradictions are described by Desmond Morris in *The Naked Ape:* "My excuse is that Homo sapiens, no matter how erudite he has already become, has nonetheless remained a naked ape; despite the mass of lofty new motives, he has lost none of his primitive base ones."[14] Morris argues that the old instincts have been with us for millions of years, while the new instincts have been with us for only a few thousand years. His description of the fundamental biological nature of humankind is very familiar to anyone who differentiates the types of brain systems represented in Figures 4-2 and 4-3. The animal is still very present in the human species.

In order to understand their customers better than before, marketers can learn a lot from *sociobiology,* the science that relates the behavior of people and animals to the biological laws. In terms of the first arrangement, we can argue that the external world probably allows easily understood signals to penetrate our consciousness, but the internal milieu can dominate the management of behavior through the way the signals are filtered and integrated. Within the parameters of the second arrangement, we can assume that communication generated in the neocortex constitutes a poor guideline for transactions—because of the minimal, limited, or at best complicated relationship with the actions generated by the limbic system.

Communication generated in the neocortex is considered digital communication, and comprises the written and spoken word. It is unique to humans in its content, its relatively recent evolution, and its capacity for dishonesty. The limbic system is responsible for analog communication, which includes posture, gestures, mimicry, and cries. It is common to both humans and animals. It comes from a more distant evolutionary stage, is involuntary (and therefore tolerates dishonesty only with great difficulty), and reflects the emotional state. The voice can be considered a mixed form. A public official stands before the microphone and claims to be furious about something, but the voice betrays the fact that this is not the case. Facial expression, particularly the eyes, can also be very revealing. For example, the eyes cannot hide disappointment with an

ASPECT	ANALOG COMMUNICATION	DIGITAL COMMUNICATION
Consists of	Cries, attitude, signs, mimicry	Spoken language Written language
Controlled by	Limbic system	Neocortex
Found in	Humans and animals	Humans
Evolutionary age	Old	New
Communicates	Emotion	Content
Trustworthiness	High, seldom lies	Can lie
Sensitive for	Images	Text

FIGURE 4-4.   Analog versus digital communication.

election defeat, even though the loser unflinchingly claims, by some complex piece of reasoning, that the loss is actually a victory. Observant TV viewers are not fooled: They can see that the politician is lying. Ultimately all communication is formed by the interaction and integration of the neocortical and limbic systems; the accent can lie on one or other of the two systems in a current transaction or in actual behavior.

The two types of communication can be represented as in Figure 4-4.

HOW NEUROLOGY CAN HELP MARKETERS

Are there conclusions to be drawn for marketing in general, and for direct marketing using new media in particular, from the two arrangements of the brain with their respective types of information and communication? One important insight is that these mental systems are the instruments that we use to make choices—or, more specifically, the prerequisites for being able to make choices. Even after the information and media revolutions, we will still be using the same mental systems. In a heuristic model, where we can work out the best options for the marketing process step by step, the following points can help us detect the relevant patterns and make the appropriate choices. They are particularly recognizable to (direct) marketers.

1. The insights gained from behavioral psychology and neurology make it easier to understand why marketing and purchasing decisions are made. The uneasy relationship between what would seem rationally obvious and the way we actually act need no longer amaze us. That's just the way we are. Nor do we have to be surprised that the same stimuli will be perceived differently not only by different individuals but also by the same person, depending on prevailing attitudes, preconceptions, moods, and beliefs.

2. The claims people make in reference to direct-marketing media ("I never read it," "I throw it all away without even looking at it," "I like getting mail")—have very little influence on how people actually behave. The perspective of neurology

helps us understand that this is a common human characteristic accentuated by the precise nature of the research, not
something specific to marketing. It's only human.

3. Analog communication—subconscious experiences rooted
in the limbic system, as well as unconscious impulses—play
a major role in human behavior. Such impulses, even if they
conflict with what can be deduced by logical reasoning or
with something that is stated explicitly, override the faculty
of reasoning. This is an important guideline for the effective
design of media. The limbic system can also be described as
a biocomputer driven by images, whether originating in the
internal or the external world.

4. Market research derived from questionnaires that seek
respondents' opinions or preferences, or ask about past or
future buying patterns, always deals with digital information
transmitted via the neocortex. As a result, not much importance about future (buying) behavior can be attached to it.
The more closely the interview setting resembles the actual
buying situation, the more reliable the results of a question-
naire will be. The problem is that creating such a setting is
usually costlier than evaluating an abstract situation.

In Chapter 2 we saw various examples of the discrepancies between reported and actual behavior (self-service stores
and cash machines). The reported behavior thus concerns
the reasoned, proposed behavior—the intention that the neocortex has generated. In these examples, it appears that the
limbic system behaves in an entirely different manner from
that intended by the neocortex. Direct marketing, in fact,
constitutes an ideal testing environment. Each medium can
be tested in an actual situation so that we can determine the
response to each of the variables. The fact that in a certain
situation such a medium serves only as a test to see how the
receiver will react is something that only the sender knows.
Reality and the test situation are the same for the person
being tested; in fact, the subject is not even aware of being
part of an experiment.

In other words, the reaction from the neocortex, which
has to be used by market research to predict what the limbic

system will do, can be sidestepped in order to measure directly the reaction of the limbic system itself. Given the extremely limited correlation between the two systems, this is an important plus.

5. The power of the marketing database, and the way in which it is constructed, is closely related to whether the recorded information is generated by the neocortex (reported information) or the limbic system (behavioral information). Because of the difference in the value of the information that these categories can have in predicting purchasing behavior, it is essential that we differentiate between them. *It is therefore of vital importance that the structure of the human brain be reflected in the structure of the database.* The advantage of behavioral or transactional information when selling via the media is that this information need not be generated separately, but can arise as an automatic part of a well-designed commercial process. The amount of behavioral and transactional information increases in proportion to the experience accumulated, so that the database grows when used.

Reported information should never be mixed in with transactional information and should generally be entered into a database separately—if it should be entered at all. Before doing this, you must carefully determine the value of the information for the commercial process. If it does not seem valuable—which is quite likely, given the complicated relationship between the neocortex and the limbic system— you have to determine the actual purpose of the information before deciding whether to add it to the database. It might be useful for operational tasks, such as opening times, the installed base, or names of contacts. But if there are no such operational objectives, you should make the courageous decision of pushing the delete button. It will do your database a world of good.

The experience of observing daily life can thus make an important contribution to successfully performing the marketing process—despite the fact that it takes place beyond the four walls of your company. Your own experiences, the experi-

ences of practical direct marketing, the results of advertising
research, and the experiences with new media create a picture
surprisingly similar to the findings of behavioral psychology,
social biology, and neurology. The contribution to a successful
marketing operation is especially important when new possibilities, as well as new uncertainties, present themselves
through the revolutions in information and media.

NOTES

1. P. A. Vroon, *Toestanden* (*Situations*), Ambo, Baarn, The Netherlands
   1993.
2. Vroon, op. cit., p. 163.
3. C. Witterman, *Competence and Performance in Belief Revision*,
   University of Utrecht, The Netherlands, 1992.
4. "A Disaster Has a Hundred Stories," discussion with Prof. Dr. W.
   Wagenaar, *Apeldoornse Courant*, December 29, 1992.
5. S. Vögele, Institut für Direkt-Marketing, D-8092 Gelting.
6. W. D. Scott, *The Theory of Advertising*, Garland, New York, 1985
   (reprint).
7. G. Meyer-Hentschel, *Erfolgreiche Anzeigen, Kriterien, und Beispiele
   zur Beurteilung und Gestaltung* (*Successful Advertising: Criteria and
   Examples*), Gabler Verlag GmbH, Wiesbaden, 1988.
8. W. Leven, "Werbestory-Recall ohne Werbeaussagen-Recall,"
   Werbeforschung & Praxis, Folge 3, 1987.
9. Th. Kok, "Het kijken naar een postordercatalogus" ("Looking at a Mail-
   Order Catalog"), in *Handboek Direct Marketing* (*Direct Marketing
   Handbook*), B5250, Samsom Bedrijfsinformatie, Alphen a/d zRijn, The
   Netherlands, 1995.
10. D. Ogilvy and others, *Ogilvy on Advertising*, Orbis Publishing Ltd.,
    London, 1993.
11. P. Postma, *Het Direct Marketing Boek* (*The Direct Marketing Book*),
    Management Bibliotheek, Amsterdam, 1990.
12. M-Marsel Mesulam, *Principles of Behavioral Psychology*, F. A. Davis
    Company, Philadelphia, 1985.
13. P. A. Vroon, *Tranen van de krokodil* (A Crocodile's Tears), Ambo,
    Baarn, The Netherlands, 1989.
14. Desmond Morris, *The Naked Ape: A Zoologist's Study of the Human
    Animal*, 1967.

THE MIX OF INFORMATION, MEDIA, AND HUMAN BEINGS

Will we still be stuck in traffic jams in the new marketing era? Will we still have to wrestle with stacks of paperwork every weekend just as we do now? And is the meeting of two world leaders still news, even though the two have been able to call each other up for years and can see each other readily? The answer to all three questions is not just yes today, but also yes in the new marketing era. Of course, technically speaking, people can work from home, but there are still many limitations, not the least of which is the fact that it is socially undesirable. Paper can be replaced by screens, but some things you will continue to want on paper and some things will have to be sent to you on paper because otherwise you won't notice them. Technically speaking, heads of state have not needed to meet for years, because they can contact each other with videoconferencing facilities whenever they want, but that sort of communication is obviously not quite good enough. You know what you can expect only if you look someone else directly in the eye.

Will we stay home to do all our shopping in the new marketing era? Will we simply send an intelligent agent out to search via the PC for the best offer available? Will we talk to screens more than to our partners, and are they likely to give us more satisfactory answers? The answer to these three questions is no and will always be no. The reason, in principle, is the same as that for answering yes to the three questions beginning this chapter: It is all possible, but that's not the way people are.

People remain people. They have for the last 50,000 years. *The computer generation's whizkids are no exception. They are a product of the times, just like the rock 'n' roll generation.* And in the new marketing era, this trend will not suddenly be reversed—even in situations where we think it might be reversed. Electronic payments are an example. Almost everybody thinks that the number of electronic payments is increasing enormously while the number of cash payments shrinks. The first idea is correct: From a minute share it increases to a very small share. But the amount of cash money, like the number of books, is bigger than ever before. What's more, the amount of cash money is even increasing. According to *American Banking,* the number of ATMs in the United States grew by 169 percent at the so-called nonbanks and by 26 percent at the largest 50 banks between 1994 and 1995. Figure 5-1 shows the number of personal payment transactions above one pound in the United Kingdom. The number of transactions with cash money shows a

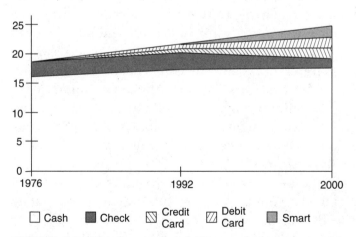

FIGURE 5-1   The future of cash. Personal payment transactions.

decreasing growth, but growth nevertheless. What's more, all other payment methods together are only a small fraction of the total. Sometimes things change less than you think. "The youth of today love luxury, are bad mannered, despise all authority, have no respect, and talk when they should work." That observation was made by Socrates in about 400 BC.

To get a good idea of the new marketing era, we have to go further than understanding information technology's capabilities and the profound changes in the media. Its essence lies in the synthesis of the results of the information revolution, the media revolution, and people. We're inclined to forget the last factor, even though we know plenty about it. The trouble is that the other two elements are undergoing a development that is undoubtedly revolutionary. Humankind is at best undergoing a very slow process of evolution—and then only in one of the three brain systems that direct behavior: the neocortex. The development of the neocortex may be seen as a wonderful process, but it is taking place over a period of tens of thousands of years. What's more—and this is something we've learned from psychology—behavior can be controlled by all manner of environmental factors, but this fact does not alter the basic desires, urges, emotions, and needs that are rooted in the older parts of our nervous system. The care of offspring, sexual needs, aggression, territorial protectiveness, the survival instinct, and socialization (e.g., the construction and acceptance of social hierarchies) are part and parcel of the human "hardware." Unlike cognitive processes, emotions display a connection with the limbic system and, just as with instincts, are difficult or even impossible to control. Even in so-called feral cases—people who have been reared by animals and who have had no contact with humans—emotions show normal human reflexes; naturally, the cognitive processes function completely differently. Reflexes such as surprise and stamping feet in anger are not learned. Emotions, actions, and instinctive behavior are to a large extent predetermined. We must take this into account.

The future depends on the way in which the three main ingredients—information, media, and people—affect one anoth-

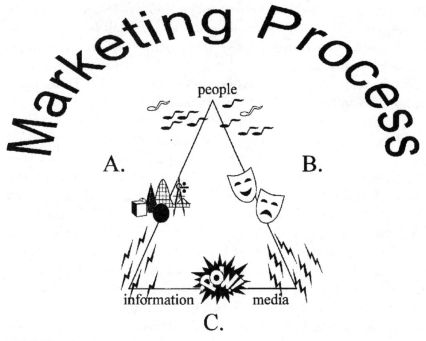

FIGURE 5-2

er. In terms of their rate of development, they are just about as far out of synch as possible. This is illustrated in Fig. 5-2. This book places the three components in the context of the commercial process. How do they affect one another in the new marking era? In the past there have been attempts to describe these commercial processes in terms of rational human behavior. In many fields of economic and marketing theory, the underlying assumption is that we are rationally driven to achieve maximum benefit. This assumption is useful for the calculation of points of equilibrium, and lends itself perfectly to differential and integral calculations in examinations. But even the slightest notion of human behavior is sufficient to understand that in purchasing situations it has very little to do with rational thinking. Complete consumer behavior models have been constructed using suppositions that appear to be logical, but bear little relation to how people actually behave. *The comeback of the celebrated "gut feeling," probably as a reaction, has to some extent become license for all manner of irresponsible action.*

In this last chapter we will examine how each of the components of the commercial process can affect the other two, and what characteristics result for the commercial process as a whole. It is a synthesis of two components that have undergone revolutionary development and of a single component that is able to learn but is essentially stable. This synthesis will ultimately dictate how the commercial environment will look in the new marketing era.

INFORMATION AND HUMAN BEINGS

The interaction between people and the information revolution—tension field A in Figure 5-2—has two important consequences in the commercial process:

- The way in which the information is presented
- The function given to information, divided into emotional and rational aspects

THE WAY INFORMATION IS PRESENTED

More and more sensations that affect our nervous system are digitalized. This means that the resulting sensations can be aroused regardless of place or time. Combined with enormous capacities—for storage, transfer, and processing with "intuitive" software—and with networks, this creates an infinite potential for influencing the spinal cord, the hypothalamus, the limbic system, and the neocortex. A note of caution: The new marketing era is about techniques that can influence the human nervous system and all the powers it has developed through evolution; thus people can still react as human beings, even to sensations that have been generated, as it were, synthetically.

As a result, the way in which information can be presented today corresponds far better to what the nervous system likes: color motion pictures with matching sound. Our nervous system adores it. The impact is much greater than with graphics or a series of numbers. It is said that people are becoming increasingly visually adjusted in our world of video images. But there are no grounds for supposing that people are adjusting differently; this visual preference has been present for many thousands of years. The fruits of the information revolution simply make it increasingly possible for people to satisfy their existing desires. Emotion and intellect can thus be played with at will, and the satisfaction of primal urges can be re-created on the spot. We will look at this topic in more detail later.

FUNCTIONS

The function of information is shifting independently of the form in which media is presented. As noted in Chapter 2, a marketing database should be used to realize maximum added value, through the Marketing Information Matrix.® In terms of how information is presented, the rational and emotional effects go hand in hand; in terms of function, they do not and can even move in opposite directions.

If we listen to the information in a marketing database instead of talking at it, we may very well expose the actual patterns of human behavior, but the discovery can come up against such emotional resistance that the facts are ultimately denied. For example, a marketing manager claims that a certain product is intended for well-educated and better-paid males. The manager then discovers that the product has as many female as male customers, and that there is hardly any distinction to be detected in the customers' level of education or income. A frequent psychological reaction in this type of situation is to think up a rationale that confirms the original point of view and that explains why things appear to be different in the database.

The information revolution offers the *possibility* of generating information that is valuable for forecasting, but this is not to say that the data will be used properly. The efficiency of the commercial process can be improved significantly only if the intellect is allowed to play a role. We expect this to be the pre-vailing scenario in the world of business-to-business and finan-cial services. If, however, a particular industry is dominated by emotional considerations, it is by no means a foregone conclu-sion that the possibility of improving commercial processes will also be experienced and recognized as such. At present, this is often the case with fast-moving consumer goods that rely heav-ily on a brand name; the managers who feel most comfortable here primarily act according to their feelings. As noted several times, emotional responses can be so strong as to prevail over scientific explanations that prove otherwise.

As we have seen, "stated behavior" can be directly con-nected to the neocortex. When asked a question, people give a reasoned answer formed in that part of the brain. The com-plex relationship between the neocortex and the limbic sys-tem, resulting in well-meaning people giving at best a rea-soned answer that does not tally with their subsequent behavior, reflects the differences between stated behavior and actual behavior. The actual behavior is a reflection of the lim-bic system, and perhaps even of phylogenetic systems—sys-tems that go back even further in evolution. In principle, these systems are unchanging, a concept that exactly matches the fact that past behavior is a trustworthy predictor of future behavior. In this way, the types of information presented here can be linked to the types of brain systems; their correspond-ing characteristics can then be seen as plausible.

When the rational approach supersedes the emotional, the management of commercial processes is strongly affected. Decisions made on arbitrary criteria, on more or less assumed feelings, and on the benefit a manager can have when making a certain choice, disappear into the background. It will then be up to list managers—using tools of statistical methods, neural networks, and whatever—to determine from the mar-keting database who is to be approached, with which product, and in what manner, in order to create the highest chance of making a sale. Management sets the policy and decides whether it wants to maximize the return on investment or expand its market share. A considered choice is made between achieving higher sales with existing clients or investing in new clients, in which case the maximum permitted payout time for a new client is indicated. The list manager then goes to work with the input. In this way, the reasoning is based, not on opinions and feelings or on personal ideas and preferences, but on the information in the database. Managerial policy can thus be far better directed at the desired marketing objectives. This more substantial function for information will cause a turnaround in management methods and problem solving. But once again, the changes apply only in companies where rational thinking is tolerated, and that is certainly not the case everywhere.

The opportunities for expert systems, marketing databases, data warehouses, and the forms of event-driven marketing are to be found in this confrontation between information and people. *It all boils down to using automated tools based on data that compensates for human shortcomings.* These tools do not take over the commercial process; they are aids to the successful management of those parts of the commercial process where people fail because of the characteristics of their own mental processes.

In terms of the form of presentation, the information revolution has an enormous potential in marketing management at the moment a prospect sees the information. The *function* of information provides a great potential for determining the optimal client/timing/product combination. When emotions allow, there are profound consequences for managing the commercial processes. But when emotions predominate, information's new function will not be used significantly, despite the possibilities available.

MEDIA AND HUMAN BEINGS

The types, quantities, and functions of media are becoming increasingly important simply because they are growing so rapidly. The same might be said of cars. The time when people asked whether medium A would "win" the race with medium

B is long past. A large number of media forms can claim a permanent place, and to a certain extent are largely interchangeable. People are prepared to be influenced by a number of different media, as long as the array offers something positive or is to their advantage.

There are, however, important limitations in tension-field B of Figure 5-2 that the spiritual fathers of some types of media overlook. The fact that something is possible does not mean that the human nervous system is tempted to do it.

MANY OPPORTUNITIES AND RESTRICTIONS

In Chapter 3, we saw how the Marketing Media Cube® shows the extent to which the functions of media have increased: In communications the new media can become personal, can offer a high level of interactivity, and are ideally suited to influencing the visual and aural senses. In addition, they lend themselves to making transactions. Although technically speaking the new media can also be used for shopping, their importance here seems exaggerated. Many shopping rituals cannot be easily imitated by a medium. If you are buying a car, you want to feel it, smell it, hear it, and drive it. Nevertheless, thanks to the media revolution, new media are not just able to spread information that appeals to rational arguments; they can also play with deep-seated emotions.

Until the start of the 1990s, it seemed as if the new media would be suitable only for collecting the rational arguments in the buying process. This concept begins to pale in light of the media revolution. Teleshopping, telebanking, teleconferencing, and e-mailing will definitely have a place in our world, but not to the extent that we will be condemned to lifelong house arrest. You won't need a dog as an excuse to go for a walk.

TYPES OF PURCHASING BEHAVIOR

It is wise to recognize that in this context there are different sorts of buying behavior. Because of the media revolution, shopping can be achieved by other methods, but there is no reason to suppose that behavior itself has changed as a result. Buying behavior can be divided into routine versus special purchases, or necessity versus pleasure; in addition, we can distinguish between those people in buying situations who go out with a purpose (active buying) and those who simply allow it to happen impulsively (passive buying). Most people recognize situations in which they allow one or other of these patterns to predominate. If you visit a trade show to gain an accurate idea of the market, or you stop at all competing stores in a shopping district before making a purchase, you are displaying active buying behavior. If you take the concept to its extreme, you will replace the old-fashioned "No door-to-door selling" sign on your door with the contemporary "No unaddressed mail" on your letterbox. You will find out the information for yourself. The intelligent agent that goes searching on the World Wide Web is an attractive alternative for active buyers. People who suppose that the manufacturer will have nothing to say in the future, because buyers will go in search of the best offer via their PC, are implicitly saying that buyers will exhibit only this kind of behavior. They confuse the form that the buying behavior takes with the behavior itself.

In my opinion, there is no reason to suppose that passive behavior—whether just rummaging around for pleasure or for the satisfaction of the "feel good" factor—will disappear in the new marketing era. On the contrary, so-called fun shopping, looking around for pleasure without really needing anything, is flourishing rather than diminishing in our prosperous society; it has become an enjoyable pastime. An intelligent agent has no function in this behavior, but that doesn't mean that the behavior will disappear. If the human mind prefers fun shopping, people will react to a direct-response commercial or an infomercial that convincingly demonstrates a product that they did not even know existed. Touch, taste, smell, and experimentation play a role in lots of buying behavior, whether it be for a fruitbasket or a car. Despite all the technical advances, this is not usually possible through the media alone.

It Is Not Just About Buying

The media's extensive potential applies to a lot more than just shopping. The new possibilities for interaction perfectly complement the brain's most basic inclinations, such as the innate attraction to play, sex, idleness, and fraud. At the point where media and people meet we have to realize that these primal inclinations will be given considerable attention. People should not be surprised by the success of computer games, the content of chatline dialogues, and the popularity of "pink services."

Getting ahead by mugging someone on the street is something that most people know well enough to avoid; but there is less resistance to carrying out a misdemeanor as the distance from the crime increases. If you can behave fraudulently using electronic means, secure in the knowledge that you will remain completely anonymous and never be traced, then you have to be solidly rooted in your neocortex in order not to do so. You have much less of a chance of being defrauded by handing your credit card to a physical person—the waiter—than by using the credit card over the Internet. Yet the waiter could just as easily misuse the number as the hacker on the Internet. The idea that the chance of fraud is smaller when there is face-to-face contact is ingrained in the human brain. We can behave like animals to each other, as long as we remain anonymous. In the protected environment of our cars, we curse other drivers in a language that we wouldn't consider using in the company of acquaintances. Security levels that are adequate in traditional financial transactions are not necessarily sufficient in the new marketing era. The new media lend themselves preeminently to fun, fraud, and frolic—more so than to teleshopping.

The Importance of Feedback

The interactive aspect of media in particular ensures feedback of people's activities. This feedback provides an important correcting action. After all, if not one single intended interaction follows, there is obviously something wrong with the medium or its design. Varying different items can help establish whether the intended interaction takes place. The corrections can thus be made according to the feedback, until a form is found that produces the intended response. The advertising world should be smacking its lips at this possibility: It is the ultimate form of accountability.

The same limitation applies here as with the function of information. Advertising by its nature is emotionally charged, and attracts people of a similar nature. Even though feedback can directly indicate that a form of expression does not achieve its aim, advertisers tend to extract a rationale from the neocortex to prove that they are right, despite an obvious mistake. If nobody reacts, they can always say that the message is good for the brand. The legitimate concern that if nobody reacts nobody heard the message, and that there can thus be no positive effect on the brand, is simply repressed. But for the company that gives the intellect some credit, the interactive potential of a medium offers an unprecedented chance to increase the effectiveness of the message by tuning in more with human perception.

What's more, the successful functioning of humans as well as animals depends on their ability to learn from previous experience. Information technology provides an enormous source of new possibilities for both marketing and research into brain functions, including memory.

INFORMATION AND MEDIA

Information and media have both developed at breakneck speed, and by progressing in relation to each other, they support and accelerate each other's development. People are no longer a braking factor in tension field C of Figure 5-2. Like the sorcerer's apprentice, people have started a process from the roots of their neocortex that is now beyond their control, for which there is no end in sight, and whose results they cannot ascertain. The following factors play a role.

OVERLAP

The mergers, takeovers, and cooperation between companies that deal with media as amusement, whether suppliers of the services (content providers) or distributors (cable and telephone companies) are sufficiently familiar. The third branch that feeds in on a large scale is information technology, especially in the amusement world. It is as if Hollywood had its own branch in Silicon Valley, the cradle of IT developments. Silicon Graphics is a company that provides hardware and software for the creation of three-dimensional, animated (film) figures: the computerized cartoon. Perhaps one day the whole movie industry will move to Silicon Valley. "Siliwood" is the term used to describe the alliance between the film and computer industries.

Jurassic Park was the first big box-office hit in which advanced IT applications played a decisive visual role. The film could not have been made without it, and in that sense is an excellent example of the liaison between media and IT. Thanks to the progress of information technology in the media, we can now watch a new Disney film every Christmas. Whole teams no longer have to work on *Bambi* for years. All it takes is a couple of basic drawings and designs plugged into the right software. With one tap of the Alt F4 key, or thereabouts, the lion literally begins to walk. That makes one heck of a difference.

To a large extent, the overlap is suggested technically by something as prosaic as the processing and storage capacity for bits and bytes. The high-density CD standard from Toshiba, Time Warner, Sony, and Philips makes it possible for a full-length feature film to fit on a single CD. This DVD, with two layers of information on both sides, has a storage capacity of 17 gigabytes, whereas a CD-ROM offers no more than 650 megabytes. This means that audio CD, CD-ROM, CD-i, and video are all merging. So is there still a difference between the TV and a PC? Incidentally, the high-density standard for the new generation of compact disks has been developed because of pressure from the computer industry. Talk about the blurring of sectors.

MUTUAL REINFORCEMENT

The overlaps, amalgamations, and mutual interests tied in with the power game between information and media seem to strengthen and accelerate their development in different ways. Clusters of companies appear that are involved in a race whose finish line has yet to be determined. The convergence of so many interests with such high market expectations seems in itself to accelerate the development process.

But there is one other factor that causes this continuous acceleration. The use of the media for economic exchange—for direct marketing rather than amusement—produces information itself. With this information the medium, with its appearance and what it offers, can be adapted to strengthen its impact. The result is more information that can strengthen the medium further. It is a self-perpetuating cycle that continues as long as there are improvements to be made. The medium's interactivity thus creates a feedback mechanism for information whereby the medium can be adapted, like an autodidactic person. In fact, this is parallel to the psychological learning process. When people receive feedback from the consequences of their behavior, they can adapt that behavior with the help of the neocortex. It is this constant feedback between the components of medium and information that strengthens both.

UNCONTROLLABLE RESULTS

The speed with which IT developments are taking place makes the results uncontrollable on various fronts. Countries that are accustomed to controlling the information offered by the media will experience difficult times. This aspect of uncontrollability can be considered positive, because it allows free access to information. On the other hand, the concentration of power that arises in the business world contains the risk of mismanagement and monopolization of information, even if it is solely for amusement.

A new social dimension is emerging for which society's centuries-old controls were not designed. While people and society attempt to restrict the expression of the most primitive, least desirable human inclinations, they are helpless if this expression consists of information distributed via electronic media. The distribution of pornographic images in print is still to some extent traceable, but even Americans can't hold back the flow of electronic images. If two innocent pictures become objectionable when they are superimposed, little can be done about it. Free distribution is not subject to ethical standards. Criminals who have some grounding in information technology can also profit in this way.

They have discovered Minitel as an excellent medium for making appointments and perfectly organizing bank robberies. Mobile phones make it easy for criminals to communicate effectively while escaping from the police. The Internet has created a range of pornographic applications that go beyond the control of law enforcement.

The relationship between information and media actually checkmates the players, even when they find it necessary to intervene. But that doesn't hold back the game. *The revolutions in media and information seem to have found each other. People have started them with their neocortex, but in their use, they cannot turn back the tide with either their hypothalamus or their limbic system. And they don't seem able to stop the race itself.*

CONSEQUENCES FOR THE MARKETING PROCESS

To what extent can we sketch the outlook for the future in the new marketing era? If the core activity in marketing management becomes the formation of relationships, how will these relationships come about? And will people still want relationships? Looking into the future is an intriguing but dangerous occupation, especially if it is done by specialists in a particular field.

DEALING WITH THE FUTURE

It is more important to predict the general direction of the future than to try to make a detailed projection. Generalizations are annoying, because most people like to know exactly what to expect. And the very people who think they know exactly how the future will turn out are usually blind to all the signs that indicate it is going in another direction. Once again, this is the familiar psychological phenomenon of rejecting anything that conflicts with personal opinion. The stronger the opinion, the greater the risk of rejection.

One of the most powerful examples of this phenomenon is the sinking of the *Titanic*. Built in an age when people thought they had discovered just about everything, and had therefore managed to conquer the elements, the idea that the *Titanic* could sink was considered ridiculous. All the signs that pointed to how wrong this vision was were jettisoned because of the principles mentioned above. Before the sinking, other ships in the area had given three signals warning the *Titanic* about an iceberg. But the *Titanic* did not reduce its speed. Why should it? The ship was unsinkable. Only when the ship was already half-filled with water, and there was no more chance of it staying afloat, did people start taking hesitantly to the lifeboats, which for the most part set off only half full. People simply did not get in, because up to the last possible moment they held on to the irrational conviction that the ship could not sink. At later hearings it was established that the capacity of the lifeboats—even if they had left the ship full—was not sufficient for all the passengers. The reason for this speaks for itself: The lifeboats were not necessary because the ship could never go down.

Given the driving forces behind the new marketing era, the information and media revolutions will not necessarily follow the course predicted by all the specialists or interested parties. There is a danger to having inflexible ideas about the future, as if it were a single track disappearing over the horizon and you were the only one who knew its destination. In these developments you must not create more certainty in your own mind than is justified by reality. The chance of success is much higher if you consider in advance the various turns that a development might take. A manual can be made with all the completely contradictory possibilities, to assess the consequences for each scenario. Be on the lookout for signs that indicate in which direction developments are moving, especially if they are not in keeping with your own ideas, because then it is most likely that you will overlook them. If the captain of the *Titanic* had behaved in this way, his ship would not be lying on the ocean floor.

A simple, but important step is to read the daily and weekly journals to establish the relevant issues. Make decisions only when absolutely necessary, keeping other choices open for as long as possible. Competition can appear from the most unexpected quarter. The biggest threat for banks is not competitive banks but retailers, telecommunications businesses, and car companies that use cards to divert the payment channels to themselves. Companies that encroach on your terrain from other market sectors, however small, play by different rules. They can at first have different standards, interests, and areas of influence, so that you overlook them as competition but later end up struggling to keep up with them. Differences in efficiency are no longer 10 or 20 percent, but are suddenly more like a factor of 2 to 4. Whereas the traditional public television production companies need a whole day to make a new show, the upstarts in the commercial sector make four a day.

TWO SCENARIOS FOR RELATIONSHIPS

As noted earlier, everything in marketing depends on relationships. Will the new marketing era be one in which, thanks to the information and media revolutions, relations between sellers and buyers develop without personal intervention? That is certainly one of the possible scenarios. From the seller's side of the market, a whole arsenal of possibilities is developing. The increased number of functions that both media and information can realize create new and unimagined possibilities within existing business patterns.

Here we touch on the subject of database-managed marketing operations—in which the new marketing possibilities, sum-

marized by the Marketing Information Matrix® in Chapter 2
and the Marketing Media Matrix® in Chapter 3, are fully
exploited. *Here we are talking about the biggest shift in the mar-*
keting world since the inception of the discipline: the shift from
thinking about a product personified by a brand name to thinking
about the quantifiable relationship with the client. In business
markets the new focus can lead to a considerable strengthening
of market control; in consumer markets it means a complete
reversal of the way in which the market is approached—a reversal that causes great difficulty for traditional brand-marketing
professionals. The trail left by the customer shows the supplier
the way. The supplier is thus furnished with a whole new cockpit full of levers to pilot the market.

At the same time, we can see that the predominance of
mass marketing, and the often self-evident preference for it in
consumer markets, is less suitable in the era of diversification
of choice, interactivity, and fragmentation of the (mass) media.
This is therefore a scenario that decidedly has to be judged in
the light of all its consequences.

The alternative scenario is just as likely. Looked at from the
customer's point of view, these revolutions present the exact
opposite challenge. Buyers do not have to attach themselves to
anything or anybody. Because of the abundance of information
and media available to them, they can find their way to the
product or service supplier that best fits their needs at any particular moment. It is up to them whether they take the supplier
or the brand into consideration. If the search process becomes
too complicated, they can employ an intelligent agent. So
active buying behavior, as we called it earlier, can also be used
to good effect in the new marketing era. Trends such as individualization and the critically aware consumer are also applicable here: Consumers are the ones calling the shots. The modern consumer works and buys at home, with a "No
unaddressed mail" sticker over the letterbox and an answering
machine screening calls. The same people who once went
shopping with the latest consumer reports in hand now sit in a
cockpit full of levers, winging their way through the forest of
suppliers more efficiently than ever before. The consequences

of this second scenario—the opposite in terms of relations and who takes the initiative—are just as powerful as the first.

Each of these conflicting scenarios, based on differing purchasing behavior, has a real chance of becoming a reality. The two could also come about simultaneously, for different product/market combinations. Those who already work in a market where client relationships are an ingredient of success have a different starting point from those who have dealt only with customers who buy impulsively or according to price, or those whose success depends on a brand name. The environment will be more competitive for everybody but will also offer more opportunities for putting policies into action. That means that the chances of survival are slimmer for those stuck in the middle. People who make explicit choices will have new possibilities to strengthen their position. Thus it will be increasingly important to decide on the exact strategy that you want to follow in the new marketing era so that you can carry it out using all means available. This strategy could very well follow the scenario that aims at customer relations. But you can also opt for the scenario that puts you in the best position to be discovered by the active shopper, whether or not with the help of an intelligent agent.

Those who opt for the first scenario must decide whether the much-praised one-to-one relationship that direct marketers achieve will also come about thanks to the new possibilities offered by media and information. Aren't real relationships cemented by face-to-face contact, shaking hands, and dining out together? In short, aren't they the result of communication from the limbic system? Of course they are. That is an important limitation for the expectations arising from the first script.

If you take a look at the stamps, points, air miles, and whatever else you collect in your wallet, it is hard to know where your loyalties lie. If I sleep in a hotel in a certain chain so often that I receive a regular customer card, do we then have a relationship? Or is it just a question of enjoying ever greater advantages if I limit myself to that chain? I even get extra air miles if I show a card from some frequent-flyer program, and if I pay with my credit card I earn even more points. The piling up leads to confusion, and a limitation of the "relationship." Because who exactly am I having this relationship with?

The core of these sorts of systems is that they restrict customer choice. Even if customers do not sense a warm relationship, the mounting benefits of a consistent choice can make them decide to use the same supplier. The system's power can be increased considerably if it is coupled with a good marketing campaign. If customers perceive the way in which they are addressed as a direct reward and recognition for their behavior, then there is an increased chance of repeated positive response from their side. The supplier manages customer behavior by connecting directly to people's greed, their inclination to be awarded benefits, or—if the supplier does it really well—by gratifying their vanity. *The principle of customer loyalty is nothing but the principle people use to teach their dogs tricks: rewarding desired behavior.* Experience teaches us that despite all the confusion with these systems, good results can be achieved in the form of increased sales.

The relationship may be more synthetic than real or human, but in many situations the result is the same. True human relationships, the crux of every business transaction, are irreplaceable—but they are not always necessary. The products of the information and media revolutions do indeed support human relationships; they compensate our shortcomings but cannot replace the human connection. How close this kind of synthetic relationship, consisting of no more than laser-printed letters with a few variables, can approach a real human relationship was illustrated to me by a letter that I encountered as marketing director of Wehkamp, the Dutch subsidiary of Britain's Great Universal Stores P.L.C.

> Dear Mr. Wehkamp:
>
> As loyal customers, my wife and I were very disappointed that we did not hear anything from you on the occasion of our fiftieth wedding anniversary. Apart from that, I was deeply hurt that I did not receive a message of condolence from you on the unhappy occasion of my wife's death. But that you also take offense with my deceased wife for not ordering anything else from you is quite intolerable.
>
> Yours sincerely,

Once again, the technological innovations thus create new possibilities for suppliers as well as buyers to do business. We also have to realize that the basic starting points for the game are not changing. The gravity that made the *Titanic* sink will not be canceled out. The economic starting points associated with human passion will not change either. But within the bounds of the basic field of play, there will be an overabundance of new possibilities for both sides. Buyers and suppliers will both have a new cockpit full of levers, so that the two scenarios have a good chance of succeeding simultaneously.

WHIZKIDS ARE NORMAL HUMAN BEINGS

Will the next generation increasingly lean toward one of these two scenarios? Is there a generation growing up with completely new behavior patterns? I see no reason to make this sweeping assumption. Naturally people in their forties are awestruck by teenagers and even young children who defeat them in the use of computers. But that is not surprising. The problems that you have to deal with at the age when you are best able to learn are the ones you master most easily. If that happens to be computers, then you learn to master them to a degree that an adult will never acquire. If it is Chinese, then you will learn Chinese as a child better than any adult could manage. You learn best about the things that you encounter in childhood.

Children as well as young animals learn the values in play that they need to survive as adults. The astonishment at the ability of children to use computers is nothing more than the age-old "Gosh! Haven't you grown!" Our development is already stuck at a point beyond which the child is still developing.

Adults can also learn, but they are conditioned differently. We have learned that we have to understand things in order to be able to work with them. That is why people explain to us that a computer consists of hardware and software, peripherals, and an operating system. If the engineering of a steam iron had been explained to us like this, ironing could have been very difficult. Children learn to work with a PC without asking any questions: If you press this, then this happens.

This is how we learned to use the phone. Toddlers can defeat adults at the game Memory, because the images are simply etched in their memory.

If a computer were as simple as a steam iron or telephone, there would not be such a marked difference between children and adults. Most software is actually so clumsy—from the point of view of the user for whom it is meant—that you need to have a considerable learning capacity to be able to use the computer as a simple typewriter. If you have to switch from WordPerfect to Word, a whole week of frustration can ensue while you adapt to the software. As a user, you would rightfully expect the software to adapt itself to you.

All in all, the whizkid is nothing extraordinary. We are all a product of the era in which we live, and that is all there is to it. Not every child is a whizkid either. It is self-evident that if you grow up with computers, you will get along fine with them. I catch a plane in the same way my parents catch a train. Nonetheless, I travel farther in the same amount of time. My children will find it just as routine to travel the world virtually, and communicate with people they have never physically met, casually selecting relevant information. But their processing capacity has not increased. The memory that they have at their disposal is in principle the same as that of a 40 year-old, and the primal urges that govern the older brain systems rule a child's brain too.

Fun, Fraud, and Frolic

Communicating by looking each other in the eye and experiencing the subtle, analog signals of the limbic system has been an essential part of human communication for tens of thousands of years. It will always be essential. *We cannot deny our biological makeup.* That is why people travel such a lot these days, despite all the virtual possibilities. They want to gain real-life experience. My whizkid colleagues want a full four-week vacation because they need to go to Vietnam or they want to trek through the Brazilian rain forest.

There is no doubt that the driving forces behind the new

marketing era will alter our day-to-day existence—lock, stock, and barrel. But the people who pompously applaud the wonderful society that is just around the corner have a one-track mind that is far too fanciful. And enthusiasts are so dumbstruck by the fascinating possibilities that they end up with a utopian glaze in their eyes.

But what can we all see happening in reality? The actual successful applications in mass markets, apart from specific professional uses, are closely associated with the familiar urges and passions of the old phylogenetic systems. The nonspecialized outsider can't miss the connection, just as with the sinking of the *Titanic*. Let us look at some of the most notable examples.

Fun.   The first and biggest success of IT and media products are none other than games. All the wonderful things that have been discovered are most successful in an application that connects with one of our primal needs: fun. The games market is worth billions, and that should not surprise us. It seems safe to predict an enormous growth: Fun and play will remain an essential need. *Whether this need will be satisfied with knucklebones and hoops or new media is only a question of form.*

But the connection with the phylogenetic systems goes deeper. Look at the content of the games. The most advanced interactive material predominantly amounts to the destruction of the enemy. The survival instinct is the most basic of human needs and finds an ideal form in the newest toys. We yelled, "Bang! Bang! You're dead!" in the school playground. The revolutions in media and information have changed little in this sense. And this was to be expected. Things that are so deeply rooted in the human brain will continue to find a way to express themselves.

Fraud.   Fraud illustrates what happens when an essential feedback mechanism is uncoupled. Fighting and war can be included in this same category. At work here is the phenomenon known as *operand conditioning,* in which behavior is strongly influenced by direct confrontation with its consequences. It applies to animals as well. Under most circumstances the majority of people will avoid expressing their aggression by murder or satisfying their avarice by theft. The direct confrontation with the consequences for the victim is a sufficient deterrent.

The explosive development of the human neocortex means that all sorts of possibilities have been thought up to appease aggression or satisfy greed, but to avoid direct confrontation with the potential victim. The feedback mechanism originates from the time when technology had not come any further than a hefty club. Then it was perfect. But now that we are able to ignite explosives from a distance, and carry out precision bombing from the air, the feedback with the terrible results is lacking. A man who doesn't have the heart to slaughter a chicken doesn't necessarily have a problem with mass warfare: It is nothing more than a computer game.

In this way, upstanding whizkids who would not even dream of robbing a bank can happily steal millions via computer systems. The distance, the anonymity, and the lack of visible consequences also turn this crime into a challenging computer game. That is why, as noted earlier, sending a credit card number via the Internet is more risky than handing a card to a waiter. The growth of the neocortex makes it possible to create all these toys, but the inhibition process is no longer able to deal with the consequences.

Frolic.   The first major breakthrough for a system of one-to-one visual communication was made in France. Although the need to look up a telephone number fueled the Minitel breakthrough, it quickly became obvious where the most substantial traffic was directed: the "pink services." Even in France, where sexual escapades are less likely to cause scandal than in England or the United States, attempts have been made to camouflage this type of activity, and regulatory steps have been taken to restrict its use.

The chatline services, whose content is no mystery for anyone who is curious about what interests people, have thus become an enormous application for electronic one-on-one communication. Whereas the satisfaction of sexual needs, originating in the oldest phylogenetic systems, used to be problematic in our complex culture and in combination with the instructions that are sent from the neocortex, here the new media create a whole new context of anonymity. During a one-month period, the search engine Yahoo! registered the most popular keywords for searches, making it very clear where the interests of Internet users lie. Just guess what the most popular word is. Yes, number-one is *sex*, with 1.5 million searches in a month. From the top 20 words, 12 are erotic— *nude, porn, adult,* and so on. And the top nonerotic word? *Chat.* Up to you to guess what type of chat Internet users may have in mind. The basic needs can go their way without interference from the neocortex. That is why computer magazines are suddenly talking about "cybergasm." I have said it already: The whizkid is nothing unusual.

In the new marketing era, the most advanced information and media applications require an increasingly specialized knowledge to make effective use of the possibilities. They will allow people to follow an emotional as well as a rational script, and a script that aims at establishing relationships as well as targeting the zapping client. In every case, it is all about the client. Following the product with its price, place, and promotion, and after branding, it is now the client who becomes important and who determines what happens. The explosion of unknown possibilities means that an organization must accurately assess where its value lies and must realize this added value with all the powers offered by the new marketing era.

The important animal characteristics that we have acquired through evolutionary development will trail us even more emphatically in generations to come. The toys that we have been able to develop with the neocortex have thus become structurally imbalanced. If we look at the applications of computer games in the commercial process, we must safeguard against the risks more than ever before. And with the anticipated use, we have to play along with those primal instincts that we share with animals, as was the case in the age when we hadn't evolved any further than using a club: fun, fraud, and frolic.

INDEX

ABOUT THE AUTHOR

Paul Postma is managing partner of Ernst & Young, one of the world's leading consulting firms, and E&Y's European Director for Marketing and Customer Relations Management. His clients include banks, airlines, oil companies, government agencies, and members of the IT industry. A reknowned international lecturer, he is the author of five books and many articles on marketing.